MW00629342

When We Don't See
Eye to Eye

When We Don't See Eye to Eye

Using the Weapon of Love to Overcome Anger and Aggression

J. DAVID PULSIPHER

Covenant Communications, Inc.

Goldfish in Separate Fishbowls Looking Face to Face © Adam Gault courtesy of Getty Images

Cover design copyright © 2014 by Covenant Communications, Inc.

Published by Covenant Communications, Inc.
American Fork, Utah

Copyright © 2014 by J. David Pulsipher
All rights reserved. No part of this book may be reproduced in any format or in any medium without the
written permission of the publisher, Covenant Communications, Inc., P.O. Box 416, American Fork, UT
84003. This work is not an official publication of The Church of Jesus Christ of Latter-day Saints. The
views expressed within this work are the sole responsibility of the author and do not necessarily reflect
the position of The Church of Jesus Christ of Latter-day Saints, Covenant Communications, Inc., or any
other entity.

Printed in the United States of America
First Printing: February 2014

20 19 18 17 16 15 14   10 9 8 7 6 5 4 3 2 1

ISBN 978-1-62108-630-7

For Dawn,
who loves a good book and helping people
(I hope this qualifies on at least one account)

Contents

Acknowledgments

IT MAY SEEM STRANGE THAT such a small book has so many people to thank. But these ideas have been gleaned from many places and honed by many influences—so many, in fact, that I confess I could not name or remember them all. To a few sources of inspiration, however, I owe specific and memorable debts. First and foremost, to God the Father, the source of all truth and beauty, and to Jesus Christ, the great exemplar of assertive love. Their words and deeds, as recorded in our sacred texts, were the principle inspiration for this book and were sources of constant wonder and amazement as I tried to understand the principles they articulated and embodied. If I somehow managed to communicate anything that is virtuous, lovely, of good report or praiseworthy, to them must go all the credit and glory.

Next, I must acknowledge two important non-LDS sources. I first heard the expression "weapon of love" from the mouth of Martin Luther King in a documentary about the Montgomery Bus Boycott.[1] I was immediately impressed with the power of the phrase, and was struck with how well it intersected with revealed truth and could be applied to well-known scriptural personalities such as King David, Daniel, the people of Ammon and, of course, the Savior of the world. I later read similar sentiments regarding the power of love in the writings of Mohandas K. Gandhi—someone who truly mastered such weapons—as I studied his life and teachings while living in India. To both I offer deep thanks for insights regarding the robust strength and possibilities of love.

I express appreciation to Brigham Young University–Idaho for its flexibility and support, and especially to my colleagues in the

---

1 "Awakenings (1954–1956)," *Eyes on the Prize: America's Civil Rights Years, 1954–1985*, episode 1, directed by Judith Vecchione (PBS, 2010), DVD.

Department of History, Geography, and Political Science. They exemplify the best kind of collegiality and scholarship, generously offering their probing questions, suggestions, and friendship. David Pigott, in particular, was invaluable in regards to French sources and translations. And also to my periodic traveling companions—John Thomas, Andrea Radke-Moss, Nathan Williams, Kyle Walker, and Robert Bird—who on more than one occasion tolerated my idiosyncratic questions and helped refine half-baked ideas as we drove across sundry landscapes. Their virtuous influence permeates these pages, making this a better book than it would otherwise be. Likewise, from his vantage point at Claremont Graduate University, Patrick Mason has been a patient tutor and friend, a consistent source of wisdom who helps me think and write more clearly.

I want to thank Vaun Waddell and the rest of the editorial board at BYU–Idaho's academic journal, *Perspective: Expressing Mind & Spirit*, during its remarkable but all-too-brief run from 2000 to 2010. The journal provided a friendly and professional forum in which some of these ideas were first explored. Most of chapter 1 and parts of chapter 3 first appeared in its pages. And over the years, Vaun has been both an inspirational editor and a true friend. Likewise, the staff at Covenant Communications has been exceptionally supportive as they shepherded this book to publication. More particularly, Stacey Owen's keen editorial eye helped curb linguistic excesses and smooth awkward prose. The language and ideas all ring better because of her.

I express deep gratitude to Sarah Schmidt, Lynette and Reed Hendricks, Richard Peterson, Holly Burton, Marta Sloan, Becca Breinholt, Carrie and Lincoln Howell, Kristin McMurray, Kathryn and Bliss Harmer, and Nancy and Jerry Pulsipher, all of whom read earlier versions of the manuscript and offered helpful criticisms, suggestions, and (above all) encouragement. I must also thank my children—Elizabeth, Andrew, Jonathan, Michael, Grace, and Katherine—for permission to share their stories and for continuing to offer me their love, even when I consistently fall far short of the principles I espouse.

Finally, there are two women in particular without whom this book would never have been started nor finished. The first is Miss Brixey (now Susan Taylor of Sunnyvale, Texas), who provided one of my earliest experiences with assertive love. As my fifth-grade math teacher, she gently, compassionately, and firmly exposed my academic laziness during a private interview one afternoon. I left that encounter in tears but also with a greater vision of my capacity and responsibility to help build the Kingdom of God. I have been trying to live up to her extraordinary expectations ever since.

The other is my wife, Dawn, with whom I have shared everything, and who has been everything to me, for over two decades. I quickly learned that while I love to talk and write about high ideals, Dawn is eminently better at *living* them. After years of listening to eccentric concepts on frequent walks and during late-night chats, she finally imposed a deadline for writing them down. Throughout the process, and our marriage, she has been a beacon of hope and possibilities. This book would never have been completed without her. And in her brilliant eyes, I continue to glimpse prospects for an ever better world—between each other, with our children, and intertwined with all the human family.

Prologue
WEAPONS OF LOVE

THE PEOPLE OF AMMON TAKE my breath away. Steeped in a culture of violence, they turned from their aggressive traditions and made a sacred covenant to bury their swords and to love their enemies—even if it cost them their lives. Then, as their enemies descended, rather than cringe in their homes waiting for some brutal end, they went out to meet them—confront them—on the battlefield, stretching themselves on the ground to pray. And their enemies slaughtered them.

But, of course, the story doesn't end there. Eventually, their enemies stopped the slaughter. When these incredibly brave people praised God as they perished, their enemies' hearts were "swollen," and they were "stung" for the murders they were committing. Casting aside their swords, they joined their former opponents in prayer. Remarkably, "the people of God were joined that day by more than the number who had been slain." Furthermore, "there was not a wicked man slain." No one died in anger that day. No one died in sin. All the movement was upward, toward God—over one thousand people literally ascended to heaven, while even more turned their hearts toward their Eternal Father.[1]

In the face of such anger and aggression, the Ammonite strategy and its results are extraordinary, even within a narrative such as the Book of Mormon that is filled with exceptional behavior. Some divine pattern, some principle of power seems to move behind the details. When I was young, I could sense it but not define it. As I've grown older and become more familiar with aggression and conflict—more subtle than swords but much too common within and between families, friends, coworkers, and communities—and as I have observed similarly astonishing behavior by equally courageous and converted people, the divine principles at work

---

1 Alma 24.

with the people of Ammon have slowly become more clear. Almost by accident, or perhaps by inspiration, the people of Ammon discovered and implemented potent principles for resisting aggression and confronting anger. In short, they learned how to fashion and wield weapons of love, the art of compassionate confrontation and resistance.

I want to learn and perfect that art. It holds the key to hope and happiness in a turbulent world because even the most peaceful life faces some anger or aggression. Free-will souls such as ours rub against one another, either by accident or design. For some of us, anger and aggression are only occasional intruders in our lives. For others, they are persistent and insistent guests. We may find ourselves at the center of the turbulence or watching from the sidelines. But regardless of the consistency, intensity, or proximity of anger and aggression, most of us share a common handicap—our greatest resources, weapons of love, remain either sheathed or only timidly employed.

This is unfortunate because the weapons of love aren't wimpy. They don't involve surrender to aggression or disengagement from conflict. Love resists. Love engages. But it resists and engages according to a different dynamic because love is the greatest force in the universe. Really. It's stronger than hate or greed or fear or malice. Most of us have glimpsed its *emotional* and *spiritual* potential, but at its most vibrant and divine, love is also material and forceful. It is a *physical* force—perhaps even a primary force that organizes and binds the cosmos—and a growing body of scientific research is cataloging its characteristics and effects. Similar to light and sound, love reverberates in tangible, measurable ways. It has physical effects on our bodies and our relationships, and its influence can be traced through our homes, our communities, and our world.

By classifying the laws of love, science is merely describing what God has been trying to teach us for millennia—love is not mystical or meek but real, even forceful, and its influence is immense. Anyone who has felt even a fraction of God's love knows it is a power to reckon with. I remember the first time I recognized it—alone in my room, sixteen years old, uncertain about God, the universe, and my relationship to either, and skeptical about my capacity to distinguish divine communication from my own emotions. But when it came, the force was unmistakably separate from me, tangible in ways I had not anticipated, and, oddly enough, sweetly familiar. His love was a consuming fire. And, as with other forms of fire, it changed a landscape—the landscape of my life. It was, above all, real. And human love is just as real with similar potential to transform lives and relationships.

Similar to other universal forces such as gravity and atomic energy, once the basic principles of love are better understood, its power can be channeled and harnessed into practical tools, even weapons, albeit in different forms than we usually imagine. A weapon of love, for example, not only resists aggression but also reshapes the conflict's dynamic and has the potential to heal its sources. It ultimately engages conflict in more divine ways—with exquisite effectiveness but also with greater compassion, creativity, and human connectedness. But as with any weapon, it requires courage—more courage, in fact, than traditional weapons. In the face of hatred, greed, selfishness, violence, and abuse, wielding a weapon of love requires incredible fearlessness. It is not for the fainthearted. There may be casualties, and there are always risks, even significant ones. But every battle strategy carries risks, and the potential rewards are so extraordinary they merit such risk taking.

Ignorance holds us back—as does fear. Fear of combat. Fear of failure. Fear of inadequacy or incompetence. Perhaps even fear of love itself—robust, strident, and forceful. But the principles behind the weapons of love are not daunting. They are not complicated or unattainably idealistic. They are simple and practical. And perfect love—rightly understood and implemented—eliminates fear.

Once we learn the principles, overcome our fear, and try assertive love, our capacity to resist aggression and constructively transform conflicts will increase. We will begin to elevate all our relationships, from our families to our neighborhoods to our workplaces and to the broader world. We will find peace and hope in the midst of discord and despair. And ultimately, as the people of Ammon, we may learn to resist our cultural traditions, discard our weapons of aggression, embrace new social dynamics, and employ assertive love in revolutionary ways. As one scientist and philosopher predicted, "Some day, after we have mastered space, the winds, the waves, the tides, and gravity, we will harness for God the energies of love. And then, for the second time in the history of the world, man will have discovered fire."[2] That is a future for which I yearn, and what follows is a rough attempt to glimpse some of love's astonishing yet practical possibilities.

---

2 Pierre Teilhard de Chardin, S. J., *Les directions de l'avenir* (Paris: Éditions du Seuil, 1973), 92.

Chapter 1
SUNSHINE & SHADE

MY WIFE AND I AGREE on most things. Financial priorities? First, pay off the house. Optimal thermostat setting? 69–70 degrees. Most engaging films? British period dramas, of course. But one ongoing "area" of disagreement (literally) is our yard. I love aspen trees. Dawn thinks they're weeds. I enjoy plenty of beds. She prefers more lawn. I want to set the basketball standard on the south side of the driveway. She fancies the north. For most of these garden-variety disagreements, we have established workable compromises, such as a small but satisfying grove of aspen I cultivate in a remote corner of the yard. But one particular area—a patch of dirt sandwiched between our patio and the back lawn—has created the greatest controversy because our visions for it are completely incompatible.

Our patio lies immediately west of our back door, where it absorbs the full blaze of afternoon sunlight. Even on the mildest summer days, it can be unbearably bright and hot. Consequently, I want to dedicate a small portion of the adjoining bed for a tree, preferably something that would eventually spread a thick canopy of shade across the patio and the back of the house, creating a space that is more compatible for social events or solitary reading. But shade, even a delicate variety, would foil Dawn's purposes because she plants our vegetable garden in that sun-drenched soil. Peas, carrots, beans, squash, onions, and tomatoes abundantly and—I must admit—attractively spill over the flagstones, where they can be conveniently weeded and harvested. The last thing she wants is shade in the very place I think we need it most, and the relatively small space I want for a tree, she prefers to dedicate to parsley and spinach.

Sunshine and shade. Both are reasonable, positive values, and yet completely incompatible. Which is more important? On the eternal scale of things, which has greater value? Well . . . neither. No one would want to live, nor be able to survive, in a world of either perpetual sunshine or endless shade. Both are valuable, but they are also mutually exclusive. We can't have both at the same time. Consequently, Dawn and I are at an impasse. We each understand, even appreciate, the value of the other's position, but neither of us has been able to convince the other to switch priorities. This disagreement has thus stretched on, unresolved, for years. Although due to the economic value of our small crop and the fact that a tree would decide the issue, the default decision has favored vegetables over human comfort, and in this respect Dawn has waged a successful war of attrition.

The goal of Zion (and marriage, for that matter) is to become "of one heart and one mind."[1] But where does that leave Dawn and me? We have one *heart* when it comes to our yard—we both want it beautiful and useable—but we do not have one *mind* when it comes to this little patch of dirt. Does our disagreement—small, but deeply entrenched—disqualify us from divine unity? Must we resolve this difference, must we both have the same priority before we can be of "one heart and one mind"? These questions are important because disagreements between honorable and virtuous people are bound to occur. Not just in minor things, such as where to plant a tree, what color to paint the bedroom, or which basketball team to support, but also in more substantial areas, such as political parties, economic philosophies, business decisions, and parenting styles. Good people with righteous desires and pure intentions may sooner or later find themselves on opposite sides of an issue, often with passionate convictions.

What then are we to do? When two virtuous people disagree on an issue and their priorities are mutually incompatible, must one automatically give in to the other? And how do we decide who will yield? Certainly one way Dawn and I could resolve our dilemma would be for me to make an executive decision. Such action might achieve *conformity*—then again, probably not—but it certainly would not foster *unity*, at least not the pure-hearted unity we both seek. We often mistake conformity for unity. But true unity cannot be achieved through authority-induced compliance that superficially papers over our differences. It must be achieved by other means.

Disagreement ≠ Contention
As unity-striving individuals, we rightly seek consensus and shun contention. But in our desire to achieve the first and avoid the second

1 Moses 7:18.

we often either invoke authority or retreat at the first sign of tension or disagreement because, as Jesus taught the inhabitants of the Americas, "he that hath the spirit of contention is not of me, but is of the devil, who is the father of contention." But are disagreement and contention really synonymous? Note the full context of the Savior's declaration. It came as Jesus instructed the Nephites regarding the correct form of baptism:

> And there shall be no disputations among you, as there have hitherto been; neither shall there be disputations among you concerning the points of my doctrine, as there have hitherto been. For verily, verily I say unto you, he that hath the spirit of contention is not of me, but is of the devil, who is the father of contention, and he stirreth up the hearts of men to contend with anger, one with another. Behold, this is not my doctrine, to stir up the hearts of men with anger, one against another; but this is my doctrine, that such things should be done away.[2]

At first glance, the Savior was resolving a question about a fundamental doctrine (baptism) and cautioning against further disputations, but what he seemed most concerned about was not necessarily that the Nephites had disagreed but *how* they had disagreed. In this case, their differences seem to have led them to "anger, one against another." And, as the Savior noted, eliciting rage or resentment is not his doctrine.

Contention, then, is not simply a difference of opinion but rather disagreement with anger. Is it possible to disagree without anger? Modern prophets and apostles have consistently counseled us to learn how to disagree without being disagreeable.[3] Unfortunately, our popular entertainment and political cultures don't provide many healthy role models. Television, talk radio, and the Internet constantly reinforce an attitude of anger toward those who disagree with our point of view. Consequently, we learn to equate disagreement with contention.

True unity cannot be achieved through authority-induced compliance that superficially papers over our differences.

But consider another model—the Quorum of the Twelve Apostles— leaders who are strong, talented, and, yes, diverse in their points of

---

2 3 Nephi 11:28–30.

3 See, for example, Gordon B. Hinckley, "Excerpts from Recent Addresses of President Gordon B. Hinckley," *Ensign* (August 1996) and Quentin L. Cook, "We Follow Jesus Christ," *Ensign* (May 2010).

view. They disagree with each other, sometimes passionately, and they are no shrinking violets. I remember an Apostle once sharing with the faculty at BYU–Idaho that when he attended his first meeting with the Twelve, he was surprised at the forcefulness of the discussion. After he sat quietly for some time, another Apostle passed him a note that read, "Welcome to the Quorum of the Twelve. Here we play hardball." The moral of this anecdote is not that disagreement is good or desirable but that *disagreement* is not necessarily *contention*. What is the difference? It seems to be the spirit in which such disagreements are approached. When a disagreement is approached in a spirit of anger or malice, it is contention. But when a disagreement is approached in a spirit of love—which is a crucial ingredient of Church councils, such as the Twelve—it can foster a dynamic creativity that helps solve problems and enhance society.

Consequently, *contention* might be more properly defined as "disagreement with enmity," while a divine approach might be described as "disagreement with love." With that in mind, note this description of righteous unity from the book of 4 Nephi: "And it came to pass that there was no contention in the land, *because of the love of God* which did dwell in the hearts of the people."[4] Thus the presence of love—rather than an absence of disagreement—may be the key to eliminating contention.

Complementary vs. Adversarial Differences

God seems to value diversity, even fundamental tension between incompatible values or priorities. We see it all around us—in our families, in our neighborhoods, in the natural world, in music, in art, in science. Diversity and tension are unavoidable. Must all differences be resolved before divine unity can be achieved? Must everyone belong to the same political party or subscribe to the same economic philosophy or have exactly the same parenting styles? Must we all think and feel the same to become "of one heart and one mind"?

Probably not, because when God set up this world, He clearly created variety and opposition. A fundamental characteristic of His Creation is that it was "divided"—light and darkness, water and dry land, day and night, male and female. And God declared "it was good."[5] Such differences might be called *complementary*. Both sides are "good." Neither

4 4 Nephi 1:15–17, emphasis added.
5 See Genesis 1, Moses 2, and Abraham 4 and 5.

is "bad." Yet they are not entirely compatible nor without a key element of tension. We cannot simultaneously experience the full light of day and the dark pitch of night. The sea cannot also be dry land. And anyone who has experienced the mystery of male-female relationships knows how profoundly different the two sexes can be. Nevertheless, these tensions can be a source of incredible creativity, in the fullest sense of the word. Brilliant palettes of color are revealed at the edge of day and night. The force of energy between sand and wave, river and rock creates some of our most sublime landscapes of coasts and canyons. And with the presence of love—deep, abiding, and true—sexual differences and gendered tensions can both create life and enrich the collective capacities of men and women.

Of course, not all differences and tensions are complementary and creative. There are others—good and evil, heaven and hell, virtue and vice—which are *adversarial.* God's original, pure creation teemed with complementary differences, but Satan soon drew God's children into adversarial differences when he tempted Adam and Eve with the forbidden fruit, that they might "know good and evil."[6] Experiencing adversarial differences is a key element of mortality, tasting the bitter that we might learn to prize the good.[7] But in contrast to complementary differences, adversarial ones embody higher and lower values—true distinctions between right and wrong. Thus, an adversarial concept of opposition is central to defining righteousness, sin, even the Atonement, and it is essential to developing moral character.

But it is a major challenge for us to accurately distinguish between differences that are adversarial and those that are creatively complementary. In other words, another aspect of our mortal education is not only to learn to discern between good and evil but to learn to recognize when we should characterize the other side of a tension as *wrong* (and consequently of lesser value) and when we need to define it as simply *different* (but perhaps equally valid). Learning to make this distinction is crucial because when we can accurately separate the two, we can harness the creative power of the complementary differences rather than mistakenly wage war against a misperceived "error" or "enemy."

Making the distinction, of course, is not always easy. Our world is awash with various differences and tensions, and whenever we find

6 See Genesis 3:1–5 and Moses 4:1–11.
7 Moses 6:55.

ourselves on one side of a tension, we have a natural tendency to identify with those who agree with us and to perceive the tension in purely oppositional terms, with our side as "right" and the other side as "wrong." This happens constantly in politics, with factions lining up in ways that usually can be reduced to a tension between *freedom* and *order*. Which is more important? On the eternal scale of things, which has greater value? Well . . . neither. Freedom without order is anarchy. And order without freedom is bondage. Both have value. Each needs the other. The "right" position is usually found in the creative tension between the two, as our society and its political discourse swing back and forth between too much of one or too much of the other. They form a complementary difference. But that hasn't kept people on one side or the other from characterizing a particular issue and tension in purely adversarial terms.

Similar tensions exist in our families, our neighborhoods, and our workplaces. In any given conflict, both sides usually represent values that are equally valid and crucial to fulfilling the purposes of the family or organization but are also fundamentally incompatible—thus, they create tensions. But even though such tensions are usually complementary, for most people the conflict will *feel* adversarial because the tension is real. To move in one direction means sacrificing elements of the other. If not, there wouldn't be tension. And because we have a natural tendency to focus on "winning," it can be difficult for people in the heat of struggle to accurately identify complementary characteristics and creative potential.

Consequently, one key to identifying a complementary difference is to step back and note that when both sides of a complementary tension are combined, they typically create a *whole* rather than an *opposition*. Male and female, joined together, form a whole, and neither is better than the other. (On the other hand, good and evil, joined together, do not form a whole. They do "need" each other in a way, since their oppositional natures help define one another, but one is clearly superior in value.) Once a complementary difference is accurately identified, it becomes easier to initiate attitudes and approaches that will unleash creative energy. But if a complementary difference is mischaracterized as adversarial, it is easy for one or both sides to attribute malice, disloyalty, or incompetence to the other. Moreover, people can unintentionally become like Laman and Lemuel, mistaking truth—even inspired, loving truth—for anger.[8]

---

8 See 2 Nephi 1:26.

Brave & Loving Engagement

As we step back from our emotional investment in a particular position and perceive the opposing side as having something with potential value—even as we hold true to our own position—it is easier to love a person with whom we are in tension. Likewise, as we develop greater love for others, we are more apt to recognize the value of their positions, even if we disagree. Creative engagement becomes more probable, and we more fully partake of the divine nature as we bravely engage our opponents in loving dialogue.

Then, surprising things begin to happen. One of the most remarkable is that we may learn that others feel as deeply inspired in their positions as we feel in ours. I first noticed this several years ago, while I was serving as a counselor in a bishopric. The other counselor and I usually agreed in our advice to the bishop, but sometimes, as I tried to listen to the Spirit, I found that the advice I gave was nearly opposite to the advice proffered by the other counselor. Was one of us out of touch with the Spirit? Perhaps. But when we compared notes on such occasions—since we loved and respected each other—we discovered that while we both seemed to have righteous desires and were living worthy to receive inspiration, we sometimes seemed to receive different messages from God. This puzzled me for a time, until the other counselor suggested that by giving nearly opposite counsel to the bishop, we were helping him to see certain issues more clearly so he could make better decisions. I highlighted certain issues. The other counselor highlighted important alternatives. Sometimes the bishop decided one way, sometimes the other, sometimes he found a compromise between the two, and sometimes a new option emerged from our deliberations. Regardless of the outcome, the seemingly contradictory spiritual signals were invaluable to his process of discernment and righteous judgment. They brought *wholeness* to the discussion.

But disagreement and confrontation cause discomfort for most Latter-day Saints, especially if they involve someone to whom we feel inferior or subordinate. A wife, for example, may suppress her opinion and simply defer to her husband's judgment because he holds the priesthood and presides in their home. Likewise, a husband may constantly yield to his wife because she seems more spiritually sensitive. But husbands and wives who suppress their opinions and simply defer to their spouses are abdicating their divine obligations to counsel together and are missing an opportunity to bring wholeness to the decision-making process. Similar opportunities exist in our neighborhoods and workplaces. Engaging our creative tensions requires initiating loving dialogue and confronting our complementary differences, even when—maybe especially when—we feel inferior or subordinate.

This can seem daunting because the dynamics of dialogue—even loving dialogue—necessarily involve negotiation and compromise, and we are not naturally prone to such dynamics when we feel inferior to or, for that matter, superior to the other party. But even God, to whom we are clearly inferior and subordinate, is more open to dialogue, negotiation, and compromise with his children than we often assume. Consider several scriptural examples where virtuous people lovingly questioned a divine decision and negotiated a different outcome: Abraham pled for the fate of the righteous remnant in Sodom and Gomorrah; Moses successfully deflected the destruction of his fellow Israelites; the servant in the vineyard convinced the Master to spare it "a little longer;" and the Brother of Jared mitigated the punishments of Babel.[9] God's willingness to engage in these negotiations should not surprise us. After all, he invites us to "reason together."[10] The key, however, is that each person who successfully negotiated a different outcome did so in a spirit of love and loyalty. Still, it must have

Husbands and wives who suppress their opinions and simply defer to their spouses are abdicating their divine obligations to counsel together and are missing an opportunity to bring wholeness to the decision-making process.

taken a remarkable amount of courage—and trust—to challenge the Lord's decision and suggest an alternative course.

In the face of our complementary differences and as we struggle with our creative tensions, this type of courage is exactly what we need most—the courage to speak in love and to listen in love when others question us. The essential balance is to act, to trust, to bravely engage our disagreements rather than avoid them. Love is the key ingredient in the dialogue, but it is also the key to finding the courage to speak in

9 See Genesis 18:16–33; Exodus 32:7–14; Jacob 5:49–51; and Ether 1:33–43.
10 Isaiah 1:18.

the first place, for "perfect love casteth out fear."[11] As we pray for and develop this love in our lives, we will develop and model the courage of loving disagreement for our families, neighborhoods, and workplaces. We will recognize in everyone a common divinity, even—and especially—in those with whom we passionately disagree. Listening in humility and love will help us focus on *what* is right rather than *who* is right and will help transform our differences into dynamic creativity that can lead to appropriate accommodations and inspired solutions.

The advantage of recognizing—even encouraging—complementary differences and creative tensions is that the inspired solutions that result are more apt to embody an appropriate balance between two positive values—freedom and order, male and female, quality and efficiency, or whatever the values might be. If we listen only to those who agree with us—if we love only those who love us—we become insulated and lean too far to one side of the tension, creating imbalance and unnecessary difficulties for any endeavor. True balance embraces and tries to lovingly accommodate both sides of every complementary difference, harnessing the energy of each creative tension. It is wholeness. It is Zion. Perhaps being "of one heart and one mind" does not mean a community in which everyone feels and thinks the same but rather is better characterized as "hearts knit together in unity and in love."[12] After all, the origin of the verb *knit* is *to knot*—to join together two separate strands that never lose their individuality even as they bend around, support, and complement each other in a dynamic whole, suspended in perpetual tension against one another.

Dawn and I may never fully reconcile our complementary differences. In fact, I hope we don't, because within our creative tensions, we can lovingly explore potential accommodations and solutions. A few summers past, for example, I found a tiny maple growing in my small aspen grove, and at Dawn's suggestion, I planted it near the patio. It's still relatively small, and the bean plants nearly smother it every year. But so far it has survived. The young tree hasn't necessarily solved or erased our different priorities regarding sunshine and shade. I don't even know if it will make it through another winter. Still, should it flourish and its shade begin to interfere with the vegetables, I may yet choose to cut it down or move it to another part of the yard, because I love Dawn and

---

11 1 John 4:18.
12 Mosiah 18:21. See also Colossians 2:2.

want her to have the comfort of her garden. And I also recognize the fact that it was she who suggested this experiment in shade as a token of her love for me.

Chapter 2
CYCLES OF CONFLICT

Two of my sons once shared a bedroom over the garage. On the whole, the arrangement worked well. The room was large, the two roommates were generally pleasant, and they both preferred to retire and rise early. But a few months in, they began to argue about their stuff. One boy spread his building blocks around the floor or piled stamp and paper airplane collections on the desk, while the other preferred a more contained and orderly approach to bedroom management. When Dawn and I occasionally asked to see their floor—the *whole* floor—they argued over who had responsibility to pick up particular toys or clothes or papers. To their credit, they recognized their relationship was fracturing, and so they approached us with a solution—divide the room.

At first they wanted a literal division, with a wall. We denied their request. So they suggested sheets. We declined again. After several other proposals, including nails and string, they finally convinced us to accept masking tape, although we restricted it to the carpet, where (we naïvely hoped) it would be easier to clean. So the boys set about dividing the room, marking a line down the middle and between their beds, and creating "neutral" zones around their common desk and closet. They also established rules concerning the fate of objects that crossed over the lines and responsibilities for cleaning the neutral zones. From our room down the hall, Dawn and I watched to see how the experiment would work.

Sure enough, within a few weeks I was in their bedroom to settle a dispute. Apparently, some of my younger son's stamp collection had somehow migrated over the line, and the older boy had confiscated them. The younger boy, in turn, had crossed over the line and seized one of his brother's books. When I arrived they were shouting insults and threats at each other. The younger one, close to tears, claimed his brother was being unfair, while the older one adamantly maintained he had acted according to the rules and therefore his brother had no right to confiscate property that had not crossed the line. I eventually talked them away from the precipice, invoking their duty to love and serve one another, and convinced them to trade hostages. But similar encounters occurred over the ensuing months—not frequently, but regularly—and the potential for conflict was constantly there.

But why? When my sons first proposed the division, they insisted it would ensure greater peace. I hoped rather than believed they were right because I saw in their behavior the beats of an ancient rhythm—a destructive cycle of conflict that seems inherent to the natural man and is reinforced by our cultural training. The cycle is simple. People draw boundaries. One side eventually crosses a boundary. The other side strikes back aggressively, evoking another aggressive response and descending into a sub-cycle of retaliation. Sooner or later one side gives in, at which point a new boundary is established or an old one is reinforced, and the cycle of conflict begins anew.

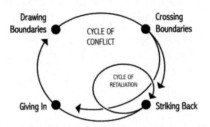

I first noticed this cycle as I taught American history at BYU–Idaho. Conflict between European settlers and the native inhabitants seemed to repeat itself again and again—different locations, different tribes, different settlers, same dynamic. Euro-Americans and Native Americans invariably began by drawing boundaries with a treaty. But no matter how well intentioned or well negotiated a treaty might have been, Euro-Americans usually violated its terms and moved across the line. Sometimes the breach was unintentional—perhaps the lines were imprecise or settlers didn't know they were encroaching on Native land. Sometimes the lines were well known, but the lure of land or the pressures of a growing population were too much. Often settlers simply saw themselves as culturally superior and above the terms of the treaty.

When Euro-American settlers crossed the boundaries, more often than not, the Natives Americans simply retreated. But sometimes they struck back, attacking settlements or wagon trains or military outposts. This strategy usually backfired because Euro-Americans usually counterattacked with even greater intensity, creating a sub-cycle of retaliation—force and vengeance employed by both groups against the other. Finally, the Native Americans surrendered, either fleeing (to Canada, perhaps) or submitting to capture and confinement. New treaties were then negotiated with more severe restrictions, thus setting up a new cycle of conflict. Euro-Americans could no longer restrain themselves and would encroach on Native land. Or Native people could no longer tolerate the constraints of reservation life and would jump the borders. And when either happened, new violence erupted.

As I tried to refine and articulate this cycle for my students, both they and I noticed something. Not only did this pattern help describe additional historical conflicts—such as those on the Korean Peninsula or between India and Pakistan—it also applied to ideological conflicts, such as those between political philosophies or religious systems. Even more strikingly, we realized the pattern was often expressed in our personal relationships—in conflicts between roommates, siblings, spouses, coworkers, neighbors, or friends.

At first we laughed, comparing the holy wars in the Middle East to the "holy wars" in their student apartments. But as I studied this pattern more closely and realized how intimately it was woven into our social fabric, how easily it was reinforced by our popular culture, and how deeply it infected or wounded people, I found it more difficult to laugh. My sons followed the cycle perfectly. But then so have I on too many occasions. Each of us, if we are honest with ourselves, has experienced—and contributed to—variations of this cycle.

Drawing Boundaries

If we look at the cycle in more detail, we can appreciate how much it affects our lives and infects our culture. We usually begin a cycle of conflict by drawing boundaries because we are natural boundary-drawing creatures. My sons' impulse to divide their room was not remarkable. Boundaries are important elements of human relations. But most boundaries are not drawn on a map. They are cultural or personal rules of behavior—sometimes subtle, sometimes explicit—that distinguish *us* from *them* or *right* from *wrong*. On a cultural level, such boundaries include language, food, clothing, art, music, entertainment, humor, and religious beliefs. Likewise, on a personal level we talk about "drawing boundaries." We permit ourselves and some people a certain type of interaction but not others. Or we allow some people into our lives and keep others out. We constantly employ boundaries to define appropriate and inappropriate behavior. They help us make sense of our world and successfully navigate its complexities.

Thus boundaries are useful, even necessary. Knowing where my yard ends and my neighbor's begins is useful, especially if I wish to be a good neighbor. Likewise, knowing what is appropriate behavior at a dinner party or when I may have "crossed the line" in playful banter with my wife is also useful (actually, essential) information. Protecting my children requires me to draw clear boundaries regarding their behavior and relationships. We need boundaries. And they usually serve us well, but only when three criteria are met—boundaries must be mutually agreed upon, mutually understood, and mutually respected.

A physical boundary imposed on one nation by another is not a formula for permanent peace. Likewise, when one person imposes all or most of the rules in a relationship, conflict is usually inevitable. When both sides feel an equal role in establishing the boundaries, they are more apt to respect them in the future. Even when we inherit pre-established boundaries—as we do when we buy a piece of land or are born into a particular culture—if we believe those boundaries were reasonably or legitimately established, we are inclined to respect them.

But boundaries must also be mutually understood. This is challenging because precision can be so elusive. Cultural boundaries are notoriously difficult to define, as are interpersonal boundaries. Every relationship (familial, romantic, ecclesiastical, professional, or otherwise) begins with an unspoken, imprecise, but necessary exploration of boundaries. Fortunately, we have well-established templates that usually help us. We gradually internalize, for example, certain patterns regarding boundaries between a "boss" and an "employee," or between "spouses" or "friends." But each relationship must establish its own unique boundaries, and the process can be excruciatingly ambiguous. Each of us probably has at least one relationship we are still trying to "figure out," by which we usually mean we are trying to comprehend its idiosyncratic boundaries.

We estimate them as best we can, but boundaries in every relationship are in constant flux and negotiation. Still, the closer both sides are to an accurate approximation, the more apt the boundaries are to be respected. But even if boundaries are mutually agreed upon and mutually understood, they still might not be mutually respected. Imperfect beings like us constantly transgress boundaries—individually or collectively, accidentally or deliberately. And when that happens, we enter the next stage of the cycle.

Crossing Boundaries

Once my sons divided their room, it was inevitable that something—a shoe, an airplane, a pencil—would eventually cross from one side of the masking tape to the other. And, of course, something did. This encroachment was accidental, but sometimes boundaries almost seem to beckon us to push or breach them. As the poet Robert Frost put it: "Something there is that doesn't like a wall."[13] Anyone who has tried to divide the backseat of a car between two squabbling children knows that one of them is likely to push his hand right up to the line, as if the line itself was calling to the child to challenge it. Some adults live that way— pushing behavioral boundaries simply because they exist. Some of us push relationship boundaries for the same reason. Perhaps a coworker is very private about her personal life, but her reticence makes us curious, so we prod anyway. Or maybe we tease a family member whom we know doesn't enjoy it because we get such a delicious reaction.

Of course, not all encroachments are deliberate. We often cross boundaries without realizing we are doing so. These may be the most frequent types of breaches, especially when we are new to a relationship and the boundaries have not yet been clearly defined. We might share too much with a new friend and embarrass her with our premature intimacy. Perhaps we ask a neighbor about his children and unintentionally open fresh wounds because he is currently estranged from them. Or maybe we stridently advocate for a policy change at work only to find it will create significant difficulties for one of our coworkers. In fact, we define boundaries more often in breaching them—and from ensuing reactions—than through any overt negotiations.

Then, of course, there are times when other people cross our boundaries, breaching behavioral lines in ways that evoke pain or embarrassment

---

13 Robert Frost, "Mending Wall," in Edward Connery Lathem, ed., *The Poetry of Robert Frost: The Collected Poems, Complete and Unabridged* (New York: Henry Holt and Company, 1969), 33.

or guilt or fear or disgust. And when we feel threatened, our fight-or-flight instinct kicks in. Do we strike back? Do we give in? Sometimes we make our choice instinctively, cultivated by years of habit. Sometimes we choose consciously because we think a particular response will bring a certain result. But neither choice brings true resolution. Both simply perpetuate the cycle in different ways.

Striking Back

When we choose to strike back, we're being violent. We usually think of violence as physical harm. While most of us have probably not participated in extreme violence, we have struck back in more subtle ways. Violence doesn't have to be physical to be painful. Some of the most damaging forms of violence are emotional or psychological. When we belittle others with insults or sarcasm or threats, we are usually responding to some perceived encroachment. They have breached some psychological or behavioral boundary—although the line was probably established without their input, their understanding, or their consent, and the breach was probably unintentional—and our verbal aggression is intended to push them back across the boundary, to keep them "in their place."

Violence doesn't even have to be overt. Taking pleasure in other people's misfortunes, ignoring them, or withholding love, financial support, or other types of assistance—all are subtle forms of violence. Anything we do with an intention to injure another person is violence. Unfortunately, it is these little wounds that we inflict most often because we don't necessarily feel violent in the process.

Of course all of us have also been on the receiving end of violence. We have breached some boundary—also probably without realizing it—then been surprised by an angry or aggressive response. When that happens, our fight-or-flight instinct kicks in, just as it does when someone breaches our boundaries. Do we strike back or give in? And when we choose to strike back, we usually force the same decision on the other person—strike back or give in to our violence? Thus the question simply bounces back and forth, at least as long as both sides keep choosing to strike back—each of us using the violence of the other to justify our own violent choices.

Meeting violence with violence creates a vicious sub-cycle of retaliation. As the Chinese philosopher Lao-tzu noted, "For every force there is a counterforce. Violence, even well intentioned, always rebounds upon oneself."[14] When my older son confiscated his brother's wayward stamps, he was using what he considered an appropriate response to resist an unjust breach of the boundary. But it led to a sub-cycle of retaliation. The younger son saw his brother's action as unfair, seized a book, and both of them began exchanging insults and threats. Each boy saw his own violence as justified. After all, hadn't the other one started it? Left unchecked and unresolved, such perceived offenses, resentments, and justifications can establish a perpetual sub-cycle of retaliation. Certain religious, political, and ethnic conflicts—such as those between Palestinians and Israelis—have become perpetual, each side seeing themselves as simply reciprocating the aggressive violence of the other. We even see it in families, as long-standing grudges linger on for decades, passed from generation to generation. Violence simply begets violence.

Giving In

So is it better to give in? Faced with anger and aggression, should we retreat? Is flight better than fight? Not necessarily. When we give in, we allow anger and aggression to have their way. We encourage future aggression by allowing violence to get results—by demonstrating that it "works." But it doesn't. Not really. When either side gives in, it simply sets the stage for another cycle of conflict because boundaries are either redrawn or reinforced. Sometimes both sides retreat, as did my sons after I intervened, but more often than not, one person has gained an advantage, meaning the other has surrendered some emotional "ground." This usually means that the person with the advantage has greater influence in defining the terms of the relationship. A berated husband or wife might submit to his or her spouse's demands. Or maybe a coworker establishes dominance even though she is officially subordinate in the company hierarchy. Perhaps a friend assumes the lead in determining all future activities. All of us know how it feels to yield to more aggressive personalities.

But giving in doesn't equal peace. When ground has been surrendered, the cycle will begin anew because the surrendered territory requires new boundaries to be drawn, and these boundaries are likely to be breached again. Even if neither side has surrendered territory, the old boundaries are simply reinforced. Once my sons gave in, they reconfirmed their existing masking tape border. But they continued to

---

14 *Tao Te Ching: A New English Version*, trans. Stephen Mitchell (New York: Harper-Collins, 1988), 30.

maintain different interpretations of the rules, thus setting the stage for future conflicts. So it is with all of us. Our cycles of conflict begin new rotations as they wait for the next boundaries to be crossed, forcing decisions to strike back or give in. They just go on and on and on—endless variations on a common theme.

A Scriptural Cycle

Such cycles can infect entire nations. We see this in the Book of Mormon, which describes centuries of cultural conflict between Nephites and Lamanites. These epic struggles began with an intimate family conflict between two brothers who drew boundaries and saw the boundaries in different ways. For Laman, the most important boundaries were those of seniority—distinctions between elder and younger, especially rights of leadership and property. As the eldest son, Laman expected deference from his younger brother. Nephi, on the other hand, placed greater emphasis on boundaries of belief and obedience. For him, the most important distinction was whether someone believed and heeded the commandments of the Lord. These competing boundaries were bound to create conflict. When Nephi began receiving visions, Laman interpreted them as a threat—his younger brother was breaching the boundary of his right to rule: "Now, [Nephi] says that the Lord has talked with him, and also that angels have ministered unto him. But behold, we know that he lies unto us; and he tells us these things, and he worketh many things by his cunning arts, that he may deceive our eyes, thinking, perhaps, that he may lead us away into some strange wilderness; and after he has led us away, he has thought to make himself a king and a ruler over us, that he may do with us according to his will and pleasure."[15]

This sense of encroachment reached a climax after their father's death when Laman and Lemuel began to contemplate extreme violence to resist Nephi's supposed ambitions: "Our younger brother thinks to rule over us; and we have had much trial because of him; wherefore, now let us slay him, that we may not be afflicted more because of his words. For behold, we will not have him to be our ruler; for it belongs unto us, who are the elder brethren, to rule over this people."[16] Nephi's response to their threat was to flee with his immediate family and his followers to another area. He took the brass plates and the Liahona, property he believed he

---

15 1 Nephi 16:38.
16 2 Nephi 5:3.

had earned through his obedience, but Laman interpreted this action as another breach of an important boundary—the boundary that defined his property rights as the eldest son.

Consequently, Nephi's flight did not end the cycle but initiated another rotation. First, new boundaries were drawn, not only in geographic terms but also in ethnic and religious ones. Those who followed Nephi called their new home the Land of Nephi while Laman and his followers occupied the land of their first arrival. The two groups began to distinguish themselves by ethnic titles (Nephites and Lamanites) and by religion (the Nephites being decidedly Christian while the Lamanites developed a form of pagan theology). These boundaries were repeatedly reinforced and modified through regular cycles of conflict.

Over time, what started as *personal* boundaries between two brothers became deeply embedded *cultural* boundaries. The Nephites saw the Lamanites as "wild" and "ferocious," a "blood-thirsty people, full of idolatry and filthiness."[17] The Lamanites, on the other hand, perceived the Nephites as "sons of a liar," a people who were repeatedly trying to "rob us of our property."[18] With such sharp boundaries in place, violence and warfare ebbed and flowed like the cycles of the tides. And not just for simply a few decades or generations but for hundreds of years.

So it is in our lives. Too often we allow the cycles of the past to determine our present and future. We draw our boundaries, cross others' boundaries, then strike back when others strike us or our own territory is threatened. We live in a culture that teaches us that "real men" (and, increasingly, "real women") never surrender. They strike back. If our "enemies" use violence, we must respond with the same ("fight fire with fire") otherwise they "win." But no one really wins. Because cycles are cycles. They almost never end.

Linear Limitations

We don't usually think of our conflicts as *cycles*, without beginnings or ends. We usually see them as *lines*, with clear origins and conclusions. A few years ago, during a backyard party, one of my sons ran up and breathlessly announced that another son was throwing apples at him. At that moment the accused boy careened around the corner of the house, clutching several apples against his stomach, his right hand cocked and

---

17 Enos 1:20.
18 Alma 20:13.

loaded. Caught red-handed—or "green-handed," since the apples were not fully ripe. Still, I asked the obvious question, "Are you throwing apples?" He looked incredulous. "He threw them at me first!" As I turned back to the first boy, he looked sheepish. But only for a moment. His expression quickly turned to indignation. "He always leaves me out!" he exclaimed. "He calls me names!" the other replied. I knew better than to press any further. I was facing a bottomless well of past injustices and former offenses from which both boys might draw infinite resources and rationalizations for their conflict. With no clear distinction between the guilty and innocent parties, I simply confiscated the apples and sent them on their way.

But who *started* the conflict? The boy who threw the first apple? Or the one who routinely excluded him from his games? Ultimately, who was to blame? Who bore responsibility? Our society frequently asks these types of questions then spends a lot of time and resources trying to answer them. If we can just find out who "started it," we believe, then a conflict will be more comprehensible. Among other things, we can sort out whose violence is "good" and whose is "bad." This is because we are born with an instinctive desire for justice and a sense that *aggressive* violence is dishonorable and wrong while *defensive* violence is honorable and right. Confronted with two people or groups throwing apples (or insults or worse), we instinctively want to identify the initial offender in order to assign the appropriate blame. If we can determine the *origin* of the conflict, we believe, the appropriate *resolution* will become clearer. In other words, once we have sorted both sides into offenders and victims, we know which outcome to root for and which side to support.

Such thinking represents a linear rather than cyclical concept of conflict. According to this model, every conflict has an origin, in which someone perpetuates an unprovoked aggression on an innocent victim. The victim can either surrender or counterattack. If a violent cycle ensues, the violence of the just defender will be noble while the violence of the unjust aggressor will be evil. But such cycles are only temporary. Eventually, the violence will end, and the linear model of conflict can imagine only two outcomes—victory or defeat—where one side must surrender to the other. According to this model, the key to achieving peaceful victory rather than tragic defeat is discovering and implementing the right formula of honorable and appropriate violence to either destroy the unjust aggressors or force them to give up.

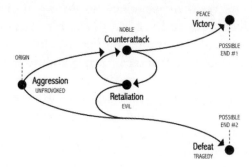

This linear model should seem familiar since it permeates our culture and provides the foundation for some of our most popular films and literature. Such stories usually begin with some harmony or balance threatened by an unprovoked threat or aggression. The heroes—be they trained professionals or just ordinary citizens—could surrender to this aggression. But of course, they don't. That would be dishonorable and tragic, and readers and audiences would rebel. Rather, the heroes choose the more honorable route, counterattacking to resist or avenge the aggression of the villains. The evil aggressors may retaliate, creating a cycle of violence, but as audiences or readers, we are trained to tell the difference between villainous violence and heroic violence. Ultimately, the hero finds the right measure and mixture of violence to defeat the villain and create a peaceful resolution in which the world is again restored to harmony and balance. There may be carnage and casualties, but in the end there is almost always peace, even if it is relatively fragile.

Peace through violence. Think how often our entertainment media reinforces this linear narrative. And we are so well trained that most of us feel cheated—and the fictional world seems unbalanced—if the villain doesn't somehow "get it" by the end of the story. The violence doesn't even have to be physical. We expect mean or greedy characters, for example, to also somehow "get their dues," usually in the form of some humiliation. Only then can an appropriate balance be restored, peace be achieved, and the conflict be resolved.

But the linear model isn't limited to our popular entertainment. It permeates our playgrounds and our business strategies. It shows up on our highways and in our politics. Through a constant barrage of examples (most of them fictional or distorted), we learn that the honorable way to resist aggression is with counterattacks, that noble violence will produce peace. As we shall see, there are more effective and divine ways to resist aggression and achieve peace, but these better options are constantly crowded out by our cultural conditioning, which urges us to counterattack. Such distorted principles subtly infiltrate our lives and color how we respond to the world and other people. We may not deliberately believe such things. But as fish in water, we are constantly awash in these concepts, and we absorb and accept their implications without realizing it. They work below the surface, emerging occasionally in bursts of anger and frustration toward someone else—a child who has misbehaved, a coworker who has encroached on our territory, or a stranger who has cut us off on the road. When that happens we inadvertently reveal how thoroughly we have absorbed the pattern. We expose those pieces of us (remnants of the "natural man") that believe violence can work and that physical, verbal, or emotional counterattacks will check aggression and construct a more balanced, harmonious, and peaceful world.

But the linear model is a myth. Violence cannot create peace. It doesn't work. It may, on occasion, *delay* a cycle of conflict. It may force a cease-fire, even a long one, but a cease-fire is not peace. Under a thin veneer of non-action, during a temporary cessation of conflict, resentments continue to smolder, biding their time, looking for the next opportunity to reignite.

Deceiving Ourselves
The linear model of violence persists in part because it contains some grains of truth. Aggression *can* be unprovoked. There *may* be times when honorable and defensive violence will protect people, at least temporarily. But we jump to these linear categories too eagerly, accepting the myth with its hollow promises of peace. As President Spencer W. Kimball observed, we are a "warlike people."[19] Armed with premature judgment and mistaken hope, we eagerly fling ourselves into cycles of conflict. And once a conflict has rotated through even just a few cycles, most participants, even well-intentioned ones, become implicated in the violence, providing more than enough blame to go around, not to mention sufficient fuel for the next rotation.

This is because we excuse our own violence by highlighting the violence of our opponents. We are right, we believe, and they are wrong. We are engaging in noble counterattacks. They are using unjust aggression

---

19 Spencer W. Kimball, "The False Gods We Worship," *Ensign* (June 1976).

or evil retaliation. Our violence will establish peace while theirs simply perpetuates misery. In our daily dramas, we almost always cast ourselves in the role of "honorable defender." We rarely cast ourselves as unjust aggressors because it is too difficult (and painful) to see ourselves that way. Even when we suspect our motives may not be pure, we can usually deceive ourselves into thinking our violence is noble by dredging up some past offense to which we claim we are simply responding.[20]

This is what my son did when confronted with the fact that he threw an apple first. For a moment he realized he had done something wrong (as revealed by his sheepish grin), but he quickly recovered, resorting to an old grievance (being left out) to justify his aggression. People who are cruel to their spouses, workers who undermine other employees, friends who give each other the "silent treatment," even muggers and scam artists who prey on innocent victims can usually find some past grievance (even if it's only remotely connected to the person they are attacking) by which they can justify their violence. Similar to the proverbial mote in our brother's eye, other people's self-deceptions are easy to identify while similar behavior in our lives go notoriously unnoticed. But we all engage in self-deception. And most of us do it fairly often.

The problem, of course, is that such behavior doesn't feel as if it's self-deception and rationalization. The grievances we dredge up and the pains we remember *are* real. And we use that pain to cloak our ambitions and convince ourselves of our own virtue. Consider Ammoron, a Nephite who became king of the Lamanites when his brother was assassinated during a secret night raid. The pain of that loss must have been keen (even if his brother was a less than reputable character), but in a letter to Captain Moroni, not only did Ammoron reference his brother's death to justify his own aggression, he reached back to even more ancient grievances to cast himself and his Lamanite warriors in the roles of noble defenders:

> I am Ammoron, the king of the Lamanites; I am the brother of Amalickiah whom ye have murdered. Behold, I will avenge his blood upon you, yea, and I will come upon you with my armies for I fear not your threatenings. For behold, your fathers did

---

20 For a thorough explanation of how easily we deceive ourselves, see Terry Warner, *Bonds That Make Us Free: Healing Our Relationships, Coming to Ourselves* (Salt Lake City: Shadow Mountain, 2001).

wrong their brethren, insomuch that they did rob them of their right to the government when it rightly belonged unto them. . . . I am Ammoron, and a descendant of Zoram, whom your fathers pressed and brought out of Jerusalem. And behold now, I am a bold Lamanite; behold, this war hath been waged to avenge their wrongs, and to maintain and to obtain their rights to the government.[21]

Did he really believe all these grievances? Captain Moroni was certainly skeptical, convinced that Ammoron had "a perfect knowledge of his fraud."[22] But all of us are capable of deep self-deception and emotional blind spots. A Nephite by birth, perhaps Ammoron did not initially believe the traditional Lamanite complaints (being robbed of their property and their right to rule), but he may have heard and repeated them so many times that he came to believe them. Even if he did not fully accept the ancient grievances, he was clearly riled by his brother's death (his blistering anger and unquenchable thirst for revenge are palpable), and he exploited that death to cloak his own violence in the cause of "justice."

Most of us don't go to such extremes as Ammoron, but we too often engage in similar self-deception, using other people's aggression—whether real or simply perceived, whether ancient or recent—to justify our own cruelty. It is helpful to remember that apostates weren't the only ones in the Book of Mormon who were seduced by false linear logic. When the sons of Mosiah proposed a mission to teach the Lamanites, most of their fellow Nephites thought the project was futile, saying:

> Do ye suppose that ye can bring the Lamanites to the knowledge of the truth? Do ye suppose that ye can convince the Lamanites of the incorrectness of the traditions of their fathers, as stiffnecked a people as they are; whose hearts delight in the shedding of blood; whose days have been spent in the grossest iniquity; whose ways have been the ways of a transgressor from the beginning? . . . Let us take up arms against them, that we destroy them and their iniquity out of the land, lest they overrun us and destroy us.[23]

Peace through violence. That is what these Nephites were advocating. Destroying the Lamanites would restore balance and harmony. They

---

21 Alma 54:16–24.
22 Alma 55:1.
23 Alma 26:24–25.

started it, and we will end it. According to this logic, violence was the only strategy that would work. The Lamanites were too "stiffnecked," delighted too much in the "shedding of blood," and spent their days in the "grossest iniquity." Always had. Always would. In other words, the Lamanites wouldn't—*couldn't*—change. If that were indeed true, the only solution really would be violence. Fortunately, the sons of Mosiah proved such thinking completely wrong.

We often entertain similar thoughts. We convince ourselves that some people will always be angry and aggressive and that the only language they understand is force. Unfortunately, such logic dehumanizes our fellow children of God. It ultimately denies the extraordinary power of Christ's Atonement because we categorize some people (whether they be angry coworkers, estranged family members, or enemy nations) as beyond the grasp of repentance, as if no one could touch their hearts, not even God. Such deceptions are tempting because the more we can make our opponents seem irredeemable, the more we can downplay their divine potential and their capacity to repent and change, the easier it is to justify our own violence against them. After all, we tell ourselves, striking back was the only way.

Thus, such false linear logic seduces us with the idea that if we can just find the right combination or magnitude of violence, we will achieve a peaceful end. But no matter how it is packaged or delivered—physically or emotionally, actively or passively—violence is not linear, only cyclical. And violence cannot break the cycle, nor establish true peace. As Martin Luther King observed:

> The ultimate weakness of violence is that it is a descending spiral, begetting the very thing it seeks to destroy. Instead of diminishing evil, it multiplies it. Through violence you may murder the liar, but you cannot murder the lie, nor establish the truth. Through violence you may murder the hater, but you do not murder hate. In fact, violence merely increases hate. So it goes. Returning violence for violence multiplies violence, adding deeper darkness to a night already devoid of stars.[24]

In a world increasingly saturated with anger and aggression, where descending spirals of conflict seem to greet us at every turn, it is possible to become discouraged or despondent. But there is a way to break the

24 Martin Luther King Jr., *A Testament of Hope: The Essential Writings and Speeches of Martin Luther King, Jr.*, ed. James M. Washington (San Francisco: HarperCollins, 1986), 594.

cycle. There is a way to confront anger and resist aggression, a way to constructively transform our conflicts. It requires us to resist an ocean of cultural training and embrace a higher law. It takes strength, determination, creativity, and above all, courage. But it is possible. And Martin Luther King understood its essential principle. For, after diagnosing the problem, he suggested the ultimate solution: "Darkness cannot drive out darkness, only light can do that. Hate cannot drive out hate; only love can do that."[25]

---

25 Ibid.

Chapter 3
A STRONGER WAY

WHEN ONE OF MY DAUGHTERS was three years old, she was obsessed with "bad guys" and peppered me with questions. Could bad guys be girls? Were bad guys fat? Did bad guys have guns? Would bad guys come into our house? Did I know any bad guys? I tried to assure her that we did not have any "bad guys" in our neighborhood and furthermore to explain that people were not so easily nor conclusively classified. But nuance is difficult for three-year-olds who want to sort everything into neat categories. And I was swimming against a torrent of popular culture (including whole genres of animated children's films) that reinforced definitive black-and-white categories.

One day I found her studying the cover of one of her favorite films—a typical fairytale with a beautiful princess, a handsome prince, and an evil villain. Pointing to the prince, who held a bow and arrow, she said, "He's nice to the girl, but he's not nice to the bad guy. I hate bad guys." Her observation stunned me because it so perfectly encapsulated one of the central lessons of such films—don't be nice to bad guys because bad guys are thoroughly and irredeemably bad. In most films the only ways to effectively resist the bad guys is either to destroy them or let them destroy themselves. You cannot change bad guys, and they will never change by themselves. Being bad is their defining character trait. Only when they are eliminated from the world will peace and harmony return.

My daughter then proposed a simple but ingenious solution— eliminate the bad guys from the film's storyline. She insisted that we needed to go to the store to purchase a version of the film without any bad guys. Despite my explanations to the contrary, she was convinced such a version existed. "They shouldn't make movies with bad guys," she said. I had to agree. I would love to see more films (especially animated children's films) without bad guys, but such versions are rare. Most films, especially the big studio blockbusters, have irredeemable bad guys. Our culture seems to crave such clear distinctions. And according to these black-and-white narratives, heroes are never "nice" to the bad guys.

"Do *you* hate bad guys?" my daughter then asked. The question stopped me short. On the one hand, I wanted my daughter to recognize evil, to be troubled by and willing to confront oppression, violence, and abuse. On the other hand, I didn't want her to jump too easily to convenient categories. Above all, I didn't want her to *hate*—to perpetuate and participate in the very thing she should be struggling against. So I tried to explain to her that we shouldn't hate anyone, even bad guys. But again I sensed my cultural handicap—one voice against a clamor of popular media that was teaching my daughter otherwise. Indeed, I found myself struggling against this cultural training and the natural man within me that soaks it up.

As I contemplate my own responses to aggression, I find strong inclinations to cheer against the bad guy, to hate those who do gross wrong, to be angry with those who injure me or, even worse, those I love. Although I am decades older, it is often as hard for me to want to be nice to bad guys as it was for my three-year-old daughter, and too often I rejoice at their demise, whether in the movies or in real life.

But here's the rub: Jesus taught us to be nice to the bad guys. "Love your enemies," He said on more than one occasion. "Bless them that curse you, do good to them that hate you." We know in our heads that this is the divine goal, but when it comes to actually putting it into practice, our hearts too often fail us and we dismiss this concept as impractical or even impossible. We tell ourselves that being kind to angry or aggressive people is simply stupid or weak. They'll walk all over us. They'll "win." Taking a cue from our cultural training (from thousands of hours of films and songs and video games), we often mistakenly believe there are only two choices when we are threatened—strike back or give it. Being nice is tantamount to giving in because the aggressor would certainly blast past our well-intentioned smiles and capture physical or emotional territory. Be strong, we say. And by that we mean strike back against aggression in all its forms.

If there were only two choices, such logic might be sound. But being nice, loving our enemies, blessing those that curse us, and doing good to those who hate us is not the same as giving in. In fact, it is quite the opposite. It is a form of resistance—intelligent, confrontational, and forceful—a third response to anger and aggression. It can be extraordinarily effective. And it is anything but stupid or weak; it is incredibly strong.

Higher & Lesser

As Latter-day Saints, we are accustomed to thinking in terms of continuums. Instead of dividing the afterlife into two dichotomous outcomes (heaven and hell) as most Christians do, we embrace a complex spectrum of possibilities (celestial, terrestrial, telestial, and outer darkness) with outcomes of higher or lesser values. This concept of higher and lesser permeates our theology. Our priesthood is divided into higher and lesser orders (Melchizedek and Aaronic, respectively). We understand the law of tithing to be a lesser expression of the higher and more comprehensive law of consecration. Even our places of worship can be classified as higher and lesser (temples and chapels). In this context, lesser does not mean "bad." In fact, a lesser law or doctrine or ordinance is usually an important stepping-stone in our eternal progression. But it is *lesser*. There is something *higher*. And God is constantly encouraging us to leave our current position, as good as it may be, and strive for something even better—something higher, stronger, more effective, and more divine.

We see this pattern in the scriptural record. God liberated the children of Israel from their bondage and gave them the law of Moses. But the law of Moses was only a stepping-stone to a more fully realized law of the gospel as taught and exemplified by the Savior during His mortal ministry. His Sermon on the Mount was saturated with references to higher and lesser:

> Think not that I am come to destroy the law, or the prophets: I am not come to destroy, but to fulfil. . . . For I say unto you, That except your righteousness shall *exceed* the righteousness of the scribes and Pharisees, ye shall in no case enter into the kingdom of heaven.
>
> Ye have heard that it was said by them of old time, Thou shalt not kill; and whosoever shall kill shall be in danger of the judgment: But I say unto you, That whosoever is angry with his brother without a cause shall be in danger of the judgment. . . .
>
> Ye have heard that it was said by them of old time, Thou shalt not commit adultery: But I say unto you, That whosoever looketh

on a woman to lust after her hath committed adultery with her already in his heart.[1]

With each injunction, Jesus encouraged His audience to move beyond the old commandments in the law of Moses—which were good—and embrace an even higher, happier, more effective pattern of living and being. With each statement, He moved the bar higher until He reached an apex with His last two enhancements of the law of Moses:

> Ye have heard that it hath been said, An eye for an eye, and a tooth for a tooth: But I say unto you, That ye resist not evil: but whosoever shall smite thee on thy right cheek, turn to him the other also. And if any man will sue thee at the law, and take away thy coat, let him have thy cloak also. And whosoever shall compel thee to go a mile, go with him twain. Give to him that asketh thee, and from him that would borrow of thee turn not thou away.
>
> Ye have heard that it hath been said, Thou shalt love thy neighbour, and hate thine enemy. But I say unto you, Love your enemies, bless them that curse you, do good to them that hate you, and pray for them which despitefully use you, and persecute you; That ye may be the children of your Father which is in heaven: for he maketh his sun to rise on the evil and on the good, and sendeth rain on the just and on the unjust. For if ye love them which love you, what reward have ye? do not even the publicans the same? And if ye salute your brethren only, what do ye more than others? do not even the publicans so? Be ye therefore perfect, even as your Father which is in heaven is perfect.[2]

With this challenge, Jesus invited His Jewish brethren to pick up and wield weapons of love. Unfortunately, His words have often been misunderstood, diluting the power of the strategy. This is perhaps most acute in the first paragraph when Jesus encouraged His audience to "resist not evil." Was Jesus suggesting that they permit evil to have its way? To allow anger and aggression to dominate? To let others abuse them? The admonitions that follow—turn the other cheek, give a man your cloak, go another mile—have sometimes been interpreted that way. But seen in another light, they are examples of lovingly confronting and, yes, even resisting evil, illustrations of a higher and more effective response.

---

1 Matthew 5:17, 20–22, 27–28, emphasis added.
2 Matthew 5:38–48.

Can turning the other cheek be an example of lovingly confronting and resisting evil? Yes, but we usually don't see it that way because we don't remember the crucial cultural context in which this example was expressed.[3] Christ's illustration was more precise than we often recognize: "whosoever shall smite thee on thy *right* cheek, turn to him the other also." Why the *right* cheek? Is that significant? He repeated this distinction when he visited the descendants of Lehi, so it must be.[4] But how? Consider the culture of the Holy Land and presumably the Promised Land as well: Ancient Jews considered the right hand to be *clean* and the left *unclean*. (Such distinctions still exist in large portions of the world, although not as strongly in European and American cultures.) Thus the implications of this example are dramatic. An ancient Jew would never use his left hand to strike someone because that hand was unclean. He would use his right. But how would a person use his right hand to strike someone else on the right cheek? By using the *back* of his hand—a demeaning gesture used only by a superior against an inferior. Someone who hit another person in this way would be trying to assert or reaffirm his domination. He might generally expect one of two responses—for the other person to cower and submit (probably the preferred response) or to strike back. Either response would help the aggressor to justify his violence. Only an inferior person would cower, so one could justify the violence as putting the other person in his proper place. On the other hand, only a violent person would strike back, so the aggressor could feel justified in using violence against a violent person.

But what would happen if a person turned the other cheek—if he presented his *left* cheek to be struck? There are only two ways an aggressor could use his *right* hand to strike another person's *left* cheek—with a fist or with an open palm. Here again, cultural context helps us understand the dynamic. An ancient Jew would only strike someone with a fist or open palm if the other person was somehow *equal* to him. Turning the other cheek thus becomes a wise, creative, and *effective* way to resist someone's attempt to dominate. Rather than cowering or striking back, this reaction gently but firmly confronts the aggressor. It says, "I will not

---

3 For the following insights regarding the Sermon on the Mount, I am indebted to Walter Wink, *Jesus and Nonviolence: A Third Way* (Minneapolis: Fortress Press, 2003). Wink's analysis is invaluable even if he sometimes seems to miss—or at least fails to emphasize—the inherent compassion and pure love in Christ's examples.
4 See 3 Nephi 12:39.

submit. Nor will I fight you with violence. But I will resist your aggression and challenge you with a choice—hit me as an equal or back down from your aggression." Either way, the aggressor's attempt to dominate has been neutralized. And if the aggressor chooses to strike anyway, he is left naked in his own violence and cowardice because the other person has neither submitted nor fought back, providing the aggressor no rationalization for his violence. Faced with his own irrational violence, the oppressor may feel shame—his heart may be "swollen" or "stung" as were those of the Lamanites who slaughtered the people of Ammon—and he may wish to repent of his unjust behavior.

Restoring the cultural context to this admonition to "turn the other cheek" thus unlocks its remarkable implications. It becomes so much more than simply allowing someone to hit us again. Through this example the Savior provided a profound example of assertive love—a more creative, more effective, and ultimately more divine response to anger and aggression. And it is anything but weak. It requires incredible courage to neither submit nor strike back but instead to meet malice with loving resistance.

A similar dynamic is revealed when we consider the cultural context of his other two examples—"if any man will sue thee at the law, and take away thy coat, let him have thy cloak also" and "whosoever shall compel thee to go a mile, go with him twain." Ancient Israel was rife with debtors and creditors, and only a very poor man might be sued for his coat. To relinquish his cloak as well would render him publicly naked in the court, gently but starkly shaming the aggressive plaintiff for his greed—an appetite so excessive that he was suing for his brother's last remnants of property. Likewise, a Roman soldier might compel a Jew to carry his pack for him, but Roman law strictly restricted this right of compulsory service to one mile. To offer to serve an additional mile was a gentle reminder of how abusive the system was, and it put the soldier in the awkward position of having to refuse the service (lest he be punished for exceeding the mile limit) thus acknowledging the humanity and equality of the person he had tried to oppress.

This pattern of more divine responses to anger, aggression, and oppression is the higher ground to which the Savior called His ancient audiences and to which He still calls us today. Love your enemies, He says. Bless them that curse you. Do good to them that hate you. Don't strike back. But don't surrender, either. Don't give in. Find similarly wise,

creative, and effective ways to break your cycles of conflict and retaliation. Learn to wield the weapons of love—the more courageous path,
the more effective method, the more celestial standard of resistance.

Justified Violence vs. Sanctifying Love

During the summer of 1833, the Lord carefully tutored Joseph Smith
in the principle of higher and lesser responses to aggression as personal
and communal violence in Missouri began to escalate and cycles of
conflict began to spiral into vortexes of abuse: "Now, I speak unto you
concerning your families—if men will smite you, or your families, once,
and ye bear it patiently and revile not against them, neither seek revenge,
ye shall be rewarded; But if ye bear it not patiently, it shall be accounted
unto you as being meted out as a just measure unto you."[5]

These instructions are fascinating and inspiring. If we do not meet
violence with violence, we will be rewarded. If we strike back, then the
violence against us is considered "just measure." In other words, the Lord
will consider our enemy's *initial* violence as a fitting punishment for the
violence we shall use in *response*. It's a fascinating idea—the punishment
comes *before* the crime. Their violence and our violence essentially
balance each other regardless of who strikes first. As a parent, I can
appreciate this model of punishment because it frees me from identifying
who "started it" and allows me to focus instead on the fact that both
sides have abused each other, and each child in a conflict has essentially
received punishment for his or her aggression from the other child. Such
is the divine arithmetic if we choose to strike back.

But if we bear the abuses patiently—and the revelation suggests we
should patiently endure at least three repetitions of violence—not only
are we promised blessings, the repeated offenses will also constitute a
testimony against our abuser:

> And now, verily I say unto you, if that enemy shall escape my
> vengeance, that he be not brought into judgment before me, then
> ye shall see to it that ye warn him in my name, that he come no
> more upon you, neither upon your family, even your children's
> children unto the third and fourth generation. And then, if he
> shall come upon you or your children, or your children's children
> unto the third and fourth generation, I have delivered thine en-
> emy into thine hands; And then if thou wilt spare him, thou shalt

---

5 Doctrine and Covenants 98:23–24.

be rewarded for thy righteousness; and also thy children and thy children's children unto the third and fourth generation. Nevertheless, thine enemy is in thine hands; and if thou rewardest him according to his works thou art justified; if he has sought thy life, and thy life is endangered by him, thine enemy is in thine hands and thou art justified.[6]

When we read these verses, we often focus on how they describe a right to self-defense. But the language surrounding this "right" is illuminating. The Lord uses the word *justified* (twice) when referring to any violent response we might make. Consequently, in order to fully understand the principles involved, we need to have a correct understanding of the concept of justification.

The word *justify* has several meanings that are relevant, including a strictly theological one: "to declare free from the penalty of sin on the ground of Christ's righteousness."[7] To be justified in Christ means to be absolved from guilt for sin, to be no longer accountable for wrong behavior. If the Lord tells us we are justified in using violence in certain situations, He is making an important distinction. Violence is still "wrong," but under specific circumstances (as outlined in the previous verses), people who engage in violence will not be held *accountable*. The sin of violence will not be held against them. They will be *justified* through Christ's Atonement. That is one of the primary purposes of the Atonement, to wipe away our sins. But, of course, the Atonement is more than justification. The Doctrine and Covenants teaches that there are actually two processes at work in the Atonement—justification and sanctification.[8]

What is the difference between justification and sanctification? As we already noted, when we are justified through Christ's Atonement, the stains of our sins are washed away. We are made white in the blood of the Lamb. But being absolved from guilt and free from penalties does not necessarily make us holy or divine. The *absence* of sin does not necessarily mean the *presence* of holiness, which is why the second process (sanctification) is so important. We hope to not only be made *clean* but also to be made *holy*. Thus the Atonement of Christ not only

---

6 Doctrine and Covenants 98:28–31.

7 Oxford English Dictionary, available at *http://dictionary.oed.com* (accessed 21 August 2013).

8 Doctrine and Covenants 20:30–31.

washes the stain of human sin from our garments, it also augments and accelerates the development of our divine character.[9]

Consequently, violence or other aggressive responses to abuse might be *justified* under specific circumstances. Nephi killed Laban. Captain Moroni rebuffed Lamanite invasions. But no matter how *justified* a violent response might be, it is difficult to imagine it could ever be *sanctifying*. We might, if we act according to divine guidelines, be held innocent of certain aggressive behavior, as Nephi and Captain Moroni certainly were. After repeated abuses by a friend or a spouse or a coworker, we might respond with *justified* anger, but such behavior can never make us holy. It cannot sanctify us. Seen in this light, striking back against aggression is a legitimate response but is it also a lesser response. There is always a higher way, for the Lord notes in the middle of his explanation about justified violence that "if thou wilt spare him, thou shalt be rewarded for thy righteousness." And not only will we be rewarded (or sanctified), but our children, and their children, and their children, and their children will also be rewarded. In other words, wielding a weapon of love will not only bless *us*, it will create ripples of positive influence as we break cycles of conflict and perpetuate dynamics of love. That is remarkable. That is divine.

So when we are confronted with anger, aggression, or abuse, we don't have just two choices (fight or flight), we have a spectrum of choices, of higher and lesser responses. In many circumstances striking back may be better than giving up, in the same way that terrestrial glory is better than telestial glory. But even striking back has higher and lesser practices. If a person feels a justified need to strike back, he could find no better model than Captain Moroni, who consistently demonstrated the highest ethics of lethal combat. He did not delight in violence, but when he felt compelled to engage in battle, it was always strictly defensive and reluctantly employed. He looked for the earliest possible moment to suspend the conflict, and once an enemy had surrendered, he offered kind and generous terms. Perhaps the best description of Captain Moroni's attitude comes from another context, the ancient Chinese philosopher Lao-tzu: "His enemies are not demons, but human beings like himself.

---

9 David A. Bednar's devotional address on the enabling power of the Atonement ("In the Strength of the Lord," 8 January 2002) describes the way in which the Atonement augments our natural abilities.

He doesn't wish them personal harm. Nor does he rejoice in victory. How could he rejoice in victory and delight in the slaughter of men? He enters a battle gravely, with sorrow and with great compassion, as if he were attending a funeral."[10]

For those who choose to strike back, whether on the battlefield or in our homes and neighborhoods and workplaces, Captain Moroni represents the highest standard. But assertive love that is pure, creative, and firm is even better. Much better. In both morality and effectiveness. Justified defensive violence may create conditions for a cease-fire, but such cease-fires are necessarily temporary because they do not fundamentally break a cycle of conflict. Forceful loving resistance, on the other hand, is a potent way to transcend such cycles, liberating both sides from conflict's destructive and dehumanizing tendencies.

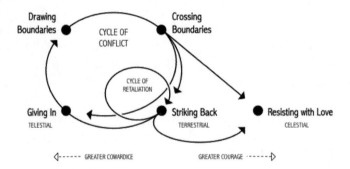

This model also highlights different degrees of courage. Striking back requires greater courage than giving up, but effectively wielding a weapon of love requires greater courage still—it requires fearlessness. To stand up to anger and aggression with justified and defensive violence, to meet steel with steel, is honorable and brave. But to meet anger and aggression with assertive love, to meet steel with character, requires even more. Mahatma Gandhi, one of the strongest advocates and practitioners of assertive love, recognized this spectrum of responses and courage: "A [forcefully loving] man or woman will and should die without retaliation, anger or malice, in self-defense or in defending the honour of their [families]. This is the highest form of bravery. If an individual or group of people are unable or unwilling to follow this great law of life,

---

10 *Tao Te Ching: A New English Version*, trans. Stephen Mitchell (New York: HarperCollins, 1988), 31.

retaliation or resistance unto death is the second best, though a long way off from the first. Cowardice is impotence worse than violence."[11]

The important lesson is that assertive love is not cowardly or weak. It is exactly the opposite because it does not surrender. It does not give in. As Gandhi once observed, those who employ weapons of love may "calmly die wherever they are but they will not bend the knee before the aggressor."[12] Assertive love *is* resistance in its highest form. And on a spiritual level, it not only leaves us guiltless (justified) but can actually help make us holy (sanctified) as we expand our capacity in this most divine of all character traits. Even more powerful is love's potential to sanctify others as well. And not just any others, but those who attack us—our enemies.

Transcending & Sanctifying

The people of Ammon seemed to sense this potential when their brethren began preparing to come against them. If we consider the normal cycles of conflict, the Lamanite aggressors were responding to what they perceived as an egregious breach of cultural boundaries. The efforts of Ammon and his brethren had brought thousands of Lamanites to reject many of their own cultural traditions, to embrace a Nephite characterization of history, and even to adopt a new name—Anti-Nephi-Lehies—to distinguish them from other Lamanites. The unconverted Lamanites saw these actions as a threat to hundreds of years of Lamanite culture and identity, and apostates such as the Amulonites and Amalekites helped stir this pot of anger and offense until it boiled over into war. Given the normal dynamics of violence, they expected the people of Ammon to either strike back (justifying the initial attack) or give in (which would also justify their violence).

But the people of Ammon demonstrated how deeply changed they had become, how thoroughly they had rejected past cultural traditions, by refusing to strike back even though they probably would have been justified in doing so. After generations of being buffeted by cycles of conflict, they chose to transcend the cycles and seek a stronger form of resistance. First, they buried their swords and other traditional weapons: "And this they did, it being in their view a testimony to God, and also to men, that they never would use weapons again for the shedding of

---

11 Mohandas K. Gandhi, *Non-Violence in Peace and War*, vol. I (Ahmedabad: Navajivan Publishing House, 1948), 148.
12 Ibid., 398.

man's blood; and this they did, vouching and covenanting with God, that rather than shed the blood of their brethren they would give up their own lives; and rather than take away from a brother they would give unto him."[13] Then, demonstrating remarkable strength and absolute fearlessness, they didn't sit in their homes and wait for the coming onslaught but rather went out to the field of battle and confronted their aggressors with the power of prayer:

> Now when the Lamanites saw that their brethren would not flee from the sword, neither would they turn aside to the right hand or to the left, but that they would lie down and perish, and praised God even in the very act of perishing under the sword— Now when the Lamanites saw this they did forbear from slaying them; and there were many whose hearts had swollen in them for those of their brethren who had fallen under the sword, for they repented of the things which they had done. And it came to pass that they threw down their weapons of war, and they would not take them again, for they were stung for the murders which they had committed; and they came down even as their brethren, relying upon the mercies of those whose arms were lifted to slay them.[14]

By neither striking back nor giving in to the violence, but rather resisting their "enemies" with faith and assertive love, they showed deep compassion and incredible faith in the divine potential of their attackers. In the process they not only sanctified their own souls, they converted (made more holy) many of their attackers.

We view the people of Ammon as highly exceptional. And unfortunately, they are. Even Ammon recognized this when he described the assertive love of his Lamanite converts and compared their responses to those of his own Nephite culture, which was still following a legitimate but lesser law of justified violence: "Has there been so great love in all the land? Behold, I say unto you, Nay, there has not, even among the Nephites. For behold, they **Assertive love *is* resistance in its highest form.** would take up arms against their brethren; they would not suffer themselves to be slain. But behold how many of these have laid down their lives; and we know that they have gone to their God, because of their love and of their hatred to sin."[15]

---

13 Alma 24:18.
14 Alma 24:23–25.
15 Alma 26:32–34.

While this episode is unusual, it is not isolated. Thousands of others have moved from the lesser law of justified violence to the higher and stronger law of sanctifying love. And while the people of Ammon provided a remarkable example under extreme conditions, the weapon they employed is used by thousands of ordinary people in ordinary conflicts. Consider the following example from Laurel Lawerence:

I grew up in a fairly large LDS family: three boys and three girls. We were far from perfect, but there was usually a good spirit in our home. But one day, we received a surprise visit from the lady next door. She came over and aired all her criticisms and gripes about our family. She expressed her disapproval that my mother expected us to do chores and also that she let us play with the Walters children across the street. (Mrs. Wood felt that the Walters children had poor manners and had not been properly trained.) She continued this harangue for some time.

My mother did not argue or even defend herself. When Mrs. Wood finally finished and went home, my mother gathered us around and told us that she knew just what to do to help us feel better. She gave us paper and pencils and instructed us each to write a list of all the things we admired about the Woods family. It was difficult at first, but gradually we got the spirit of it. After our lists were complete, my mother surprised us by collecting them and taking them next door to the Woods family. I don't remember the neighbors treating us with rudeness ever again. My sister and I learned from my mother's example, and some weeks later we made a cake and brought it to these neighbors.[16]

As did the people of Ammon, Laurel's family avoided the more typical responses—defending their behavior or giving in to her aggression by retreating inward to nurse their wounds and resentments. Similar to the people of Ammon, this family employed forceful, loving resistance, which transformed the conflict and broke the cycle.

Both the people of Ammon and Laurel's family also provide a striking example of how a higher and stronger response to anger and aggression can sanctify all it touches, even our enemies. The Savior is the ultimate example of this. When Peter smote off the ear of Malchus in

---

16 As quoted in Becky Thomas, "Don't Model Your Parenting After Laman and Lemuel," *Deseret News* (24 January 2010), available at *http://www.deseretnews.com/article/705376562/Dont-model-your-parenting-after-Laman-and-Lemuel.html?pg=all* (accessed 21 August 2013).

the Garden of Gethsemane, Jesus responded, "Put up again thy sword into his place: for all they that take the sword shall perish with the sword. Thinkest thou that I cannot now pray to my Father, and he shall presently give me more than twelve legions of angels?" Christ probably would have been *justified* in requesting the protection of heavenly warriors, but He was striving for something higher—something stronger and more *sanctifying*—and He reminded Peter of this: "But how then shall the scriptures be fulfilled, that thus it must be."[17] He allowed himself to be taken, bruised, beaten, scourged, mocked, and crucified. But He never gave in to the violence. He never surrendered to his abusers. Rather, He responded to their vitriol with extraordinarily assertive love, even at the bitter end when He cried out, "Father, forgive them; for they know not what they do."[18] And through this loving, strong, and courageous act the Savior opened the path of sanctification to everyone, even to His enemies. Thus He invites all of us to join Him on this more divine ground—to exert greater strength and courage to break the cycles of conflict in which we find ourselves repeatedly spiraling. He has shown us the way. Striking back may at times be justified, but it is not the higher law. The celestial response is assertive love.

My own capacity for assertive love is still weak. Perhaps you feel the same. But even though it may be impossible for us to achieve robust perfection as Jesus did, it is a standard toward which you and I can constantly strive. And as with other celestial laws, such as the law of consecration, we can begin within our families and with other personal relationships. As Henry B. Eyring once observed: "We begin to practice in the family, the smaller unit, what will spread to the Church and to the society in which we live in this world."[19] That is a wildfire I would love to help start. Perhaps then, when this higher law of assertive love has spread to our society and the world, I will be able to take my daughter to a store to purchase more films without "bad guys." Better yet, perhaps we will be able to find more films in which bad guys are not destroyed but confronted with weapons of love and consequently transformed for the better.

---

17 Matthew 26:51–54.
18 Luke 23:34.
19 Henry B. Eyring, "The Family," *Ensign* (February 1998), 10.

Chapter 4
ABIDING POWER

OUR BACKYARD IS NOT PARTICULARLY large, but it is a great place for imaginative play. Children can leap from boulder to boulder, or hide behind dogwood bushes and raspberry canes transformed into fortresses or caverns filled with dragons and goblins and wizards. From the kitchen window I love to watch the neighborhood children darting in and out of our garden nooks. And when I'm working in the garden, I love to listen as they negotiate the rules of their fantasy world—a process that often takes more time than the game itself. The biggest snags usually involve the supernatural powers each character will have. One child wants power over water. Another fire. A third lobbies for the ability to control animals. The most important principle for a successful game is to balance the superpowers so one child doesn't have an unfair advantage or disadvantage. But the children want as many powers as they can get or at least the "coolest" ones.

I understand their interest in power. As a child I dreamed of flying. Or being invisible. Or having X-ray vision. Most children (and many adults) yearn to transcend their physical limitations. Most of us would love to wave a wand and accomplish phenomenal things. We love the idea of power—the ability to control things. As we grow older, we may become more practical, but we never really lose our fascination with power. Instead of superheroes, we become obsessed with star athletes who exhibit exceptional physical abilities. Or we follow politics. Or movie stars. The world is filled with expressions of power—musical, economic, emotional, military, spiritual—and most of us have at least one type of power that we study well. We have an innate desire to manage our own destinies and influence the world around us, so we imitate our favorite examples of strength and power, although most models of power have crucial limitations.

One of my sons, for example, decided that he wanted to achieve world domination (don't ask *me* where this ambition comes from), and he took the Roman Empire as his model. He admired the Roman technique of conquering another culture, a carrot-and-stick approach in which potential subjects were offered a choice—they could either join the powerful and enlightened empire and become full citizens or face annihilation from a massive and well-trained Roman army. But when he tried to implement this pattern with his brothers (with too much stick and not enough carrot), they chafed under his authority and sought protection from another power—me. I tried to explain to him that such strategies are eventually doomed. The Roman Empire, impressive as it was, did not last forever. Their techniques did achieve remarkable power, but they could not endure.

My son wasn't alone. At some point, most of us have been seduced into imitating models of power that appear effective but are ultimately unsustainable. Raw physical strength, negative consequences, positive incentives—all of them are transitory. Once the threat or inducement is gone, the power evaporates. Consequently, if we want *enduring* influence, perhaps even *everlasting* and *eternal* influence, we may want to consult other models. And there is no better example of everlasting influence—what we might call *abiding power*—than God.

Divine Power
Our cultural training influences our sense of divine power. Fantasy films, for example, usually translate supernatural powers into visual forms similar to fireworks or electricity. Hence, when we think of divine power, we often imagine it as a physical force flowing from someone's hands. According to this image, God or his prophets stretch forth their hands and power flows from them to push the elements and organize the universe. This image is also scriptural. Moses lifted his rod and stretched out his hand to divide the Red Sea. Nephi reached out and shocked his brothers. And the most important tokens of Christ's Atonement are expressed in His hands—"I have graven thee upon the palms of my hands."[1] Anyone who has felt the earnest energy of a priesthood blessing knows the power that can flow through holy hands.

But hands are not the only symbol of God's power. The scriptures refer even more frequently to another conduit—His mouth. God's power is his *word*, repeatedly described as "quick, and powerful, and sharper

---

1 Exodus 14:15–22; 1 Nephi 17:54–56; and Isaiah 49:16.

than any twoedged sword."[2] It is the force by which He organized the universe and created the earth. "God said, Let there be light: and there was light."[3] This is astonishing power—God speaks and the elements obey.

> For behold, the dust of the earth moveth hither and thither, to the dividing asunder, at the command of our great and everlasting God. Yea, behold at his voice do the hills and the mountains tremble and quake. And by the power of his voice they are broken up, and become smooth, yea, even like unto a valley. Yea, by the power of his voice doth the whole earth shake; Yea, by the power of his voice, do the foundations rock, even to the very center. Yea, and if he say unto the earth—Move—it is moved.[4]

Of course, not everything (or rather, every*one*) moves. Mormon reminds us that God's own children are "less than the dust of the earth" because, in contrast to the elements, they do not always obey when God speaks: "Behold, they do not desire that the Lord their God, who hath created them, should rule and reign over them; notwithstanding his great goodness and his mercy towards them, they do set at naught his counsels, and they will not that he should be their guide."[5]

What, then, is the difference between the elements and us? In short, we are beings who can act for ourselves rather than be acted upon. Moral agency creates a different power dynamic than physical force. Free-will hearts and minds such as ours cannot be moved by electricity or gravity or even supernatural powers. God cannot compel our obedience. We must *choose* to follow.

It is a principle of divine power that we often forget. If God cannot compel his own children's hearts, neither can we. As much as we might sometimes wish otherwise, we can't simply speak and be obeyed. Other people must *choose* to follow our words. And sometimes, maybe even often, they don't. We may try to force obedience, and through intimidation or enticement we may even imagine we have achieved some success. But such success can be only fleeting. It cannot abide. Consider the following exchange, which is, unfortunately, too typical of my parenting:

"Son, you need to clean everything off your bedroom floor and vacuum it."

---

2 See Hebrews 4:12; Doctrine and Covenants 6:2, 11:2, 12:2, 14:2, and 33:1.
3 Genesis 1:3.
4 Helaman 12:8–13.
5 Helaman 12:6–7.

"Why?"

"Because it hasn't been vacuumed in several weeks, and it's time."

"Why?"

"Because the floor is dirty, and your room needs to be clean."

"Why?"

So it goes. He probes my logic. I provide a reason. He continues probing. Eventually, in exasperation, I pull out the inevitable and (I hope) unassailable reason: "Because I said so." This answer sometimes (but not very often) ends our debates. But regardless of its effect, the answer is unsatisfying, not only for my son but also for me. It ultimately begs the question, why *do* I want this child to do what I ask? "Because I said so" seems so hollow, so selfish, so arbitrary. And yet I still resort to it. Most of us do. And probably more often than we should. We want to speak and be obeyed. After all, doesn't God do this? Didn't he command Abraham to sacrifice Isaac? And wasn't the answer to the inevitable "Why?" simply, "Because I said so"?

Yes, but even God employs such answers sparingly. And when He asks us to obey without explaining all the reasons, He always grounds that request on a firm foundation of love and trust that He has already established. We then choose to follow His words, even inexplicable requests, because we love and trust the tradition upon which they are built. Consequently, if we want to achieve such enduring influence in the lives of other people, we must learn how to build a similarly sure foundation in our relationships.

Enduring Influence

True power, abiding power, is established according to simple but strict principles. The Lord taught Joseph Smith, "No power or influence can or ought to be maintained by virtue of the priesthood."[6] Until a few years ago, I focused on the second part of that sublime insight, that no power *ought* to be maintained by virtue of the priesthood. This was fairly easy to grasp—a person shouldn't simply appeal to his authority, even priesthood authority, to get other people to do things. But then I noticed the first part—not only *shouldn't* power be maintained by virtue of the priesthood, it *couldn't* be maintained by virtue of the priesthood. Even the priesthood, the power of God, cannot override agency. Perhaps the priesthood can maintain its power and influence over the elements,

---

6 Doctrine and Covenants 121:41.

things that are *acted upon*. It is, after all, the power by which the world was organized. But when it comes to power and influence over things that can *act*, such as people, even the priesthood cannot coerce our consent.

All power or influence within free-will relationships thus hinges on this principle of consent. Power requires consent. We only have power in other people's lives if they consent to give us that influence. There are many ways we might try to secure this consent, but often we employ either punishments—do this or else that—or rewards—do this and receive that. Both punishments and rewards appeal to people's emotions. Punishments appeal to fear while rewards appeal to hope. Both are effective. We use them all the time in our families, neighborhoods, and workplaces. And they aren't necessarily bad. God himself appeals to both our fears ("repent, lest I smite you") and our hopes ("a blessing, if you obey") to motivate us to follow His commandments, to consent to His power and influence in our lives.[7]

But both punishments and rewards are lesser motivations because they are necessarily transitory. The consent they generate, the power they exert, cannot be maintained. And God is constantly trying to move us to higher motivations. Consider Satan's influence in the world. He is actually quite adept at both punishments and rewards (albeit distorted and counterfeit ones) as he seeks our consent to give him power in our lives. With Moses, he employed threats, crying with a loud voice and ranting upon the earth as he tried to intimidate Moses into worshipping him.[8] With Jesus, he tried rewards, dangling the treasures of the earth and promising, "All these things will I give thee, if thou wilt fall down and worship me."[9] In both cases he failed. He did not win the consent of either of these paramount personalities. But unfortunately, he enjoys millions of smaller victories every day with similar tactics. The power he achieves, however, is transitory. The consent he obtains through bribery and extortion cannot be maintained; his influence will die. But God's endures.

This is why, as with other lesser principles, even righteous punishments and rewards are mere stepping stones to higher motivations, to more abiding power. My use of punishments and rewards is clumsy at

---

7 Doctrine and Covenants 19:15; Deuteronomy 11:27.
8 Moses 1:19.
9 Matthew 4:9.

best. But even if I eventually learn to effectively and righteously employ such tools to motivate my children, I could not use them forever. As my children grow, I want their motivations to mature as well. If they choose to obey me, if they continue to allow me to influence their lives, I do not want them to submit simply because they fear some punishment or hope for some reward. Rather, I want them to consent because they love me and have learned to trust my judgment.

This is divine influence. This is abiding power. A power Satan cannot obtain. He may temporarily win our consent through fear but not through love because he hates us. He may even momentarily win our consent through counterfeit enticements but not through trust because he is the "father of lies."[10] So he cannot appeal to our higher motivations nor achieve enduring power. God, on the other hand, works to move us to higher motivations, eventually winning our love and trust. Thus His power is potentially endless and eternal.

How does He win that love and trust? How can we do the same? As Joseph Smith learned, true and abiding consent can be obtained "only by persuasion, by long-suffering, by gentleness and meekness, and by love unfeigned; by kindness, and pure knowledge."[11] When these elements are present, our authority flows naturally and freely. And if we appeal to our authority (as we occasionally must, though it ought to be rare), we bring to that appeal a history of love and truth to bolster our claim, a foundation of trust. When God asked Abraham to sacrifice his son, it wasn't Abraham's first experience with God nor were such eccentric requests characteristic of their past relationship. Through a lifetime of experience with God and His angels, Abraham knew Jehovah was true, faithful, and loving. Abraham knew God fulfilled His promises. Isaac himself was living proof of that. So when God asked him to make this sacrifice, Abraham had a solid foundation of truth and love upon which he could trust this seemingly incongruous command. He loved God, and he knew God loved him. "Because I said so," was therefore enough, although it may not have been if that phrase had been the only basis of their relationship, if it had not been backed up with these other qualities—persuasion, gentleness, long-suffering, sincere love, kindness, and pure knowledge—repeatedly demonstrated through previous experiences.

Such power endures. We know it does because most of us have experienced it at one time or another through people to whom we gladly

10 2 Nephi 9:9.
11 Doctrine and Covenants 121:41–42.

give our consent to influence us, to whom we willingly submit because they exemplify these qualities. My father is such a person. Although he has never been a physically powerful man, his tenderness, honesty, and charity have exerted enormous influence on us, his children. We listened to him as children because we trusted his love and experience. He rarely appealed to fear. In fact, he despised coercion in all its forms. Nor do I remember lots of enticement. His strength was his character, but his influence was (and is) profound. For such people (and there are many) such power is effortless. Their lives fulfill this remarkable promise: "The Holy Ghost [a source of power] shall be thy *constant* companion, and thy scepter [a symbol of power] an *unchanging* scepter of righteousness and truth; and thy dominion [an evidence of power] shall be an *everlasting* dominion, and *without compulsory means* it shall flow unto thee forever and ever."[12]

Influence through Renunciation

Jesus summed up the essential formula of power when He said, "He that findeth his life shall lose it: and he that loseth his life for my sake shall find it."[13] Those who selfishly seek to control other people shall lose influence, while those who shed selfish ambitions will find their influence grow continually stronger. One of the best examples of this principle is George Washington. By any estimation, he was an ambitious man. He suppressed his love for another woman in order to marry the richest widow in Virginia, thus becoming one of its largest landowners. He unsuccessfully sought a commission in the British army but was elected to the Virginia House of Burgesses. As a leading figure in Virginian government and with military experience in the French and Indian War, he was the natural choice to lead the Continental army when hostilities broke out with England. After the war, he presided over the convention that produced a new constitution, then became the first president elected under its expanded national powers. In many ways his life was a long study in the dynamics of power.

In contrast to other early American luminaries such as John Adams, Thomas Jefferson, and James Madison, Washington did not bring a formal education to his study of power. Rather, he seems to have had an instinctual sense of its mechanisms. As one historian observed, Washington's "genius was his judgment," which "derived from his

---

12 Doctrine and Covenants 121:46, emphasis added.
13 Matthew 10:39.

elemental understanding of how power worked in the world."[14] And what Washington grasped better than most was that giving up traditional forms of power gave him greater influence.

A crucial moment came at the end of the Revolutionary War, when Washington's reputation was flush from his victory at Yorktown. Many of his loyal officers, including Alexander Hamilton, toyed with the thought that the new nation would be better off if Washington marched his troops to Philadelphia, dispersed the squabbling and incompetent Congress, and declared himself king (or something equivalent). After all, wasn't this the pattern of successful revolutions, especially with republics such as Rome and the British Commonwealth?

> Even while the war was still raging there had been critics in the Congress and the state governments who conjured up troubling comparisons between the Continental army and the Roman legions of Julius Caesar or the New Model Army of Oliver Cromwell. Everyone knew that these earlier experiments with republicanism had ended in military dictatorships. . . .

> Oliver Cromwell had not surrendered power after the English Revolution. [And in future years] Napoleon, Lenin, Mao, and Castro did not step aside to leave their respective revolutionary settlements to others.[15]

Generals seize power after revolutions. That was the pattern both before and after Washington. For someone as ambitious as he, the possibility of such power must have been tempting. But the genius of Washington's judgment was that he realized that both the young republic and his reputation would suffer if such a scheme were carried out. Nevertheless, even without Washington's approval, a plot for a military takeover began to form among his officers in the spring of 1783. The officers scheduled a meeting to coordinate their plans. Washington ordered that meeting cancelled and called for another meeting to be held at the Newburgh Cantonment, where he gave the most important speech of his career.

> Washington appealed simply and honestly for reason, restraint, patience, and duty—all the good and unexciting virtues.

> And then Washington stumbled as he read. He squinted, paused, and out of his pocket he drew some new spectacles.

---

14 Joseph J. Ellis, *His Excellency: George Washington* (New York: Alfred A. Knopf, 2005), 271–272.
15 Ibid., 138–139.

"Gentlemen, you must pardon me," he said in apology. "I have grown gray in your service and now find myself growing blind."

Most of his men had never seen the general wear glasses. Yes, the men said to themselves, eight hard years. They recalled the ruddy, full-blooded planter of 1775; now they saw . . . a big, good, fatherly man grown old. They wept, many of these warriors. And the Newburgh plot dissolved.[16]

Washington was sufficiently wise to recognize that true power came from a different dynamic than military force. This principle had become so engrained in his character that he was able to diffuse his officers' plot by showing *weakness* rather than strength. As Neal Maxwell observed: "George Washington could have railed at these lesser military leaders. . . . He could have harangued and threatened to quit. In a moment of near defeat, it was more than the tactic of a soft answer turning away wrath. Washington's whole character was placed on the line, and the tamed officers knew it."[17]

Washington's gesture wouldn't have worked if he hadn't laid a solid foundation regarding his character and his love. But he had, and it did. Nine months later, Washington symbolically surrendered his sword to Congress, retiring from public life. The world watched in fascination. King George III presciently (and perhaps enviously) observed that if the Revolutionary general could really turn his back on political power, he would be "the greatest man in the world."[18] And

Those who selfishly seek to control other people shall lose influence, while those who shed selfish ambitions will find their influence grow continually stronger.

that was exactly how the American people saw him. Consequently, Washington did not really give up power—he *gained* it. The American people trusted him even more after his retirement than they did when he was their hero general.

Paradoxically, Washington did not retire to gain political power but to ensure his reputation. He expected to live out his days at Mt. Vernon as a private citizen with his reputation permanently secured,

---

16 Bart McDowell, as quoted in Neal A. Maxwell, *Meek and Lowly* (Salt Lake City: Deseret Book, 1987), 26.

17 Ibid.

18 As quoted in Ellis, *His Excellency*, 139.

but his deep sense of duty brought him out of retirement (twice) to use (and risk) his enormous influence—once to preside over the Constitutional Convention, and again to become the first president under its new provisions. Each time, the trust he had earned through his voluntary retirement was crucial to the survival of the new nation. The American people trusted a new government with strong authority because they knew the man who oversaw its creation was someone who could be relied on to keep his ambition in check and lead them safely into an uncertain future. As Thomas Jefferson described it, the power of Washington's character and reputation allowed him to preside over the tumultuous birth of a new nation "until it had settled down into a quiet and orderly train."[19] For all of these reasons, Washington is known as the "indispensible man" in the birth of American liberty and government. His example of restrained ambition still reaches across generations and engenders our trust. As one historian has noted, Washington's choices "gave us a whole new definition of greatness, which was renunciation of power, not the embrace of it."[20]

Another remarkable leader who discovered and exemplified this essential principle was Mohandas Gandhi. His entire life became an experiment in renunciation and power. He never held any government office or wielded official power, but millions followed him. He owned no property and cared nothing for it, so he could not be bribed or blackmailed. He counted his own life as naught, so he could not be threatened or intimidated. He bridled his passions so no one could appeal to his appetites. In short, he was incorruptible, thus the people loved and trusted him. When he spoke, they obeyed. When he fasted, they changed. They knew he loved them. So he was powerful—abidingly powerful—as were the "armies" of men, women, and children who followed him.

The Book of Mormon also illustrates this principle of power. King Benjamin was loved and respected by his people because he restrained his authority and labored to support himself rather than burden the people with heavy taxes. His son, Mosiah, followed his example of discipline and went even further—abolishing the monarchy, relinquishing family control of the government, and establishing an

---

19 Letter to Dr. Walter Jones, 2 January 1814.
20 Richard Norton Smith, in "Are We to Be a Nation?" *Liberty: The American Revolution*, episode 6, directed by Ellen Hovde and Muffie Meyer (PBS Paramount, 2004), DVD.

independent system of judges to rule the people and protect their liberty. The result? Well, the people of Zarahemla adored him:

> And they did wax strong in love towards Mosiah; yea, they did esteem him more than any other man; for they did not look upon him as a tyrant who was seeking for gain, yea, for that lucre which doth corrupt the soul; for he had not exacted riches of them, neither had he delighted in the shedding of blood; but he had established peace in the land, and he had granted unto his people that they should be delivered from all manner of bondage; therefore they did esteem him, yea, exceedingly, beyond measure.[21]

Thus, as did George Washington, King Mosiah laid a foundation of enduring influence based on love and restraint. When he suggested a new form of government, the people of Zarahemla trusted him, followed his advice, then celebrated his name for generations, illustrating again that those who renounce traditional forms of power—those who "lose" their lives—find even greater influence than before. The paradox, of course, is that most people who achieve power through renunciation are not necessarily seeking greater influence. They are usually just doing what they feel is right and good. But by doing so, they enhance their authority. In the words of the ancient Chinese philosopher, Lao-tzu, "The Master doesn't try to be powerful; thus he is truly powerful."[22]

Personal Power
To gain influence by renouncing power seems counterintuitive to most people, a seemingly contradictory truth that is difficult for most of us to grasp, let alone implement. But it works. One of the most dramatic Book of Mormon examples of this principle did not involve political power but rather personal influence, the kind of influence most of us seek in relationships. Before Mosiah abolished the monarchy, his sons had already renounced their rights to the throne, turning their back on political power altogether and pursuing instead a life of missionary service among the Lamanites. The second son, Ammon, went to the court of King Lamoni. Did Lamoni know who Ammon was or the political power he had renounced? Perhaps. The scriptural record isn't clear. But Lamoni did offer his daughter as a wife to Ammon (a remarkable proposal, considering the Lamanite's traditional antipathy

---

21 Mosiah 29:40.
22 *Tao Te Ching: A New English Version*, trans. Stephen Mitchell (New York: HarperCollins, 1988), 38.

for the Nephites), so he may have recognized Ammon's royal lineage and may have been trying to establish a political alliance through marriage.

Regardless, Ammon declined Lamoni's proposition and offered instead to be his servant, voluntarily descending even farther from his previous status as a prince, becoming now a shepherd and a stable hand—an extraordinary example of renunciation. Through Ammon's subsequent faithful and cheerful service, Lamoni learned how much he could trust this former prince. Therefore, when the humble servant proposed a radical change to Lamoni's view of the world, one that upended the Lamanite's traditional historical narrative, the king was inclined both to listen and to follow. He willingly consented to give Ammon tremendous influence in his life and in the lives of his people—not political authority but *spiritual* power, mightier and more abiding than a crown.

A similar dynamic occurs on an even more intimate scale in our relationships. Several years ago I noticed my relationship with my thirteen-year-old son—an honest, pure, hard-working young man—was beginning to fray. Despite his good character, we seemed to butt heads more frequently. I was increasingly frustrated at his resistance to (and sometimes disgust with) my parental decisions. But as I stepped back to look at the dynamic, I realized my pride was getting in the way, creating a dynamic in which I was increasingly becoming locked in a power struggle with my son. Part of the conflict was due to my son's understandable teenage impulse to establish an independent identity, but I was having a difficult time acknowledging his more mature (and thus more equal) status. In my attempts to influence my son, I was appealing in a direct and formal way to my parental authority: "Because I said so." Too often this was my only defense to his probing queries of my logic. And with each arbitrary assertion of my authority, I was losing influence.

To regain that influence, I had to let go of my pride, and with it the false security of my authority. So rather than reminding him of our hierarchical relationship, I began to look for occasions to acknowledge his equality or even his superiority. He is, for example, confident in social situations in ways I never was, especially at his age. I sought opportunities to serve him rather than assert my role as his father. And, predictably, as I treated him with greater equality, respect, and love, he treated me the same but also, paradoxically, with greater *deference*—more frequently seeking my advice and listening to my counsel. By letting go of my authority, I had gained influence.

In the midst of this transition, my son taught me a valuable lesson about trust. One point of conflict was late-night phone calls. He liked to talk—a lot—but his time began to exceed hours I thought courteous or wise. His mother and I imposed a ten-o'clock phone curfew, but I had to badger him with repeated reminders to get off the phone at the right hour. One night I poked my head into his room at ten minutes to the hour. "Ten more minutes," I reminded him.

"Okay, Dad."

I gave him twenty. At ten minutes past, I couldn't wait any longer and headed down the hall, where I could still hear his voice. He saw me coming. "Just getting off," he said, hanging up.

"Too bad," I said casually. "You missed a great opportunity to earn trust points."

I'm not even sure where the idea came from, but it hit home. He lifted his head and sat up. "What are those?"

"You earn them when you do things without being reminded."

"So I lost points?"

"No, because I didn't really expect you to get off without a reminder. You just missed an opportunity to earn some." And I left him with a puzzled look on his face.

A few days later, he cornered me. "So how many trust points do I have?" he asked.

"Oh, there isn't an exact tally," I explained. "You're either earning them or losing them. And at some point you earn enough that we know we can trust you with more privileges and responsibilities."

The idea caught his fancy. He eagerly took every opportunity to point out when he was earning them. I came home one night from a late meeting, and he greeted me at the door. "Off before ten!" he declared, raising the phone so I could see. I smiled and gave him a high five. I rarely had to remind him of the curfew again.

But the lesson I learned wasn't simply a cute parenting tip. Rather, the experience taught me something more valuable—not only does my son earn or lose trust points, I am also constantly earning or losing trust points. Everyone does. When Washington surrendered his sword to Congress and when Ammon offered himself as King Lamoni's servant, they earned major trust points. Likewise, when I am consistent, reasonable, respectful, and loving—when I renounce my selfish ambitions and pride, let go of the formal levels of power, and focus on persuasion, gentleness, long-suffering, sincere love, kindness, and pure knowledge—my children return my love and trust with their own. And my influence grows, not only with my children but also with my wife, my friends, my coworkers, and anyone else with whom I relate.

Such power is ultimately central to God's influence in the hearts of His children. We follow Him because we trust Him. We willingly consent to His direction and influence because we know several fundamental truths about Him: God is perfectly restrained in His power, never interfering with our agency. He is perfectly constant, "the same yesterday, today, and forever."[23] And He is perfectly benevolent with a deep and abiding love. So we respond to His restraint, His reliability, and His charity with our own love, trust, and (ultimately) self-restraint. The Apostle John beautifully encapsulated this essential principle when he said, "We love him, because he first loved us."[24]

Granting & Revoking Consent

I only have power or influence in other people's lives if they consent to give it to me. Likewise, other people only have power in *my* life if I consent to give it to them. At its most fundamental level, this principle works for good or evil in our lives, depending on whom we choose to give our consent. God only has power in my life if I let Him. And Satan only has power in my life if I let him, which is why the prophets continually encourage us to *choose* whom we shall serve, to choose who will influence our lives. It is a choice we make over and over. And not just between the influence of God and Satan. We also repeatedly grant other people influence in our lives, although we usually don't see it as a choice. Consider how often you have heard or said or thought, "They made me [happy, angry, etc.]" Such statements are expressions of our *consent*, demonstrating that we have chosen to give other people power over our emotions—for better or worse. But such statements also reveal our self-deception, implying we had no agency. We didn't *choose* to feel or act this way, we tell ourselves, *they* did. They "made" us. But we always have a choice—that is both the joy and the burden of moral agency.

We choose who has power in our lives. We can grant it to those we love and trust. But we can also revoke it from those who intend us harm, refusing to be intimidated or provoked. This is the essential principle

---

23 Mormon 9:9.
24 1 John 4:19.

Victor Frankl identified from his experience in a Nazi concentration camp:

> The experiences of camp life show that man does have a choice of action. There were enough examples, often of a heroic nature, which proved that apathy could be overcome, irritability suppressed. Man can preserve a vestige of spiritual freedom, of independence of mind, even in such terrible conditions of psychic and physical stress.
>
> We who lived in concentration camps can remember the men who walked through the huts comforting others, giving away their last piece of bread. They may have been few in number, but they offer sufficient proof that everything can be taken from a man but one thing: the last of the human freedoms—to choose one's attitude in any given set of circumstances, to choose one's own way.[25]

Frankl's insight may be summarized thus—we cannot control what other people do, but the one thing no one can take away from us is how we choose to respond to what others do. When we give in to their anger, aggression, or abuse, we allow them to control us. Consequently, if such tactics have achieved power over us, we have forged our own chains. We have consented to our own oppression. Gandhi understood this principle as he struggled to awaken his countrymen to the power within them to throw off British rule. "Even the most despotic government," he said, "cannot stand except for the consent of the governed," and when "the subject ceases to fear the despotic force, his power is gone."[26] Unfortunately, he noted, "most people choose rather to yield to the will of the tyrant than to suffer for the consequence of resistance."[27]

Anger and aggression can only hold power in our lives if we allow them. But Gandhi's simple solution for India holds the same promise for our intimate oppressions: "The moment the slave resolves that he will no longer be a slave, his fetters fall. He frees himself and shows the way to others. Freedom and slavery are mental states. Therefore, the first thing is to say to yourself; 'I shall no longer accept the role of a slave.'"[28] This is

25 Victor Frankl, *Man's Search for Meaning* (New York: Washington Square Press, 1985), 86.
26 Mohandas K. Gandhi, *Young India*, (30 June 1920), 3.
27 Ibid., (9 June 1920), 3.
28 Mohandas K. Gandhi, *Harijan* (24 February 1946), 18.

not a principle just for political resistance but for intimate relationships as well. The moment we decide that we will no longer be cowed by another person, our emotional fetters dissolve.

On the other hand, if we strike back against anger and aggression, if we respond with verbal, emotional, or physical violence, we are still allowing others to control us because they are dictating the terms of the exchange. We have allowed ourselves to be drawn into behavior we would not normally condone. We have become similar to them. Granted, striking back may be better than surrendering because when we strike back they have *less* control, but they still have *some* control and far more than they should. Unfortunately, it is by *our* consent (by allowing ourselves to be provoked) that they have obtained this influence.

So both choices (giving in and striking back) grant too much influence to anger and aggression, but assertive love refuses to play by their rules. It revokes our consent, eliminating both fear and anger. Alma taught these essential principles of power to his people when they lived in the land of Helam. First he taught them to be careful about whom they allowed to influence their lives.

We choose who has power in our lives. We can grant it to those we love and trust. But we can also revoke it from those who intend us harm.

He knew how quickly they could enslave themselves if they gave their consent to the wrong people:

> And now as ye have been delivered by the power of God . . . out of the hands of king Noah and his people, and also from the bonds of iniquity, even so I desire that ye should stand fast in this liberty wherewith ye have been made free, and that ye trust no man to be a king over you. And also trust no one to be your teacher nor your minister, except he be a man of God, walking in his ways and keeping his commandments.[29]

But when the priests of King Noah and the Lamanites stumbled onto their secluded community, Alma's people were tempted to fear, to give the wandering army power by allowing it to intimidate them: "But Alma went forth and stood among them, and exhorted them that they should not be frightened, but that they should remember the Lord their God

---

29 Mosiah 23:13–14.

and he would deliver them. Therefore they hushed their fears, and began to cry unto the Lord that he would soften the hearts of the Lamanites."[30]

Under his guidance, Alma's people responded to this violent threat without fear or anger but rather with assertive love, showing the armies of the lost Lamanites how to find their way back to their homes and families. And while these Lamanites betrayed Alma and his people by returning and physically enslaving them, their spirits were never captured or conquered. When those rulers threatened death as punishment for verbal prayers, the people found creative ways to lovingly resist, by praying in their hearts.[31] In other words, they never gave their full consent to their would-be rulers, and so those rulers could never achieve abiding power.

Power requires consent. This is an essential principle regarding weapons of love, and subsequent principles hinge on it because the key dynamic of assertive love consists of revoking our consent from harmful forms of power and building enduring power through trust and compassion. The point isn't to become completely independent of other people, even abusive people. Such isolation is neither possible nor desirable. We want to be open to righteous influences, and we want our lives to be intertwined with others' in healthy and nurturing ways. With assertive love we can resist unrighteous dominion, remove our consent from destructive relationships, and through our resistance, ultimately transcend and heal those relationships. Nothing is more liberating. Nothing asserts and protects our spiritual freedom more effectively.

Nothing is more powerful.

---

30 Mosiah 23:27–28.
31 Mosiah 24:11–12.

Chapter 5
EXERTING FORGIVENESS

ALBERT WHITE HAT WAS BORN on the Rosebud Lakota Reservation in South Dakota. Until he was seven, when he began a formal institutional education, he spoke only the Lakota language and followed traditional Lakota ways. "I grew up with a lot of the older people," he said, "and listened to the stories. And those stories were inside of me." During the late 1950s, when he was sixteen, he entered the St. Francis Jesuit Mission School, a boarding school on the reservation, where he was taught to be ashamed of his Lakota language and heritage. Unfortunately, this was a common philosophy within the Indian boarding school system— educators believed they must "kill the Indian" to "save the child." School officials cut the children's hair short, forbade them from speaking their tribal languages, and dressed them in Euro-American clothes—all in a well-intentioned effort to prepare them to be successful in a "white man's world." But more often than not, the children became trapped between two worlds—partially trained in both, fully at home in neither. This is what happened to Albert White Hat.

In the late 1960s, he decided to return to the traditional Lakota ways. He grew his hair long, began speaking his language, and embarked on a series of vision quests—spiritual journeys facilitated by intense fasting and meditation, usually in some remote landscape. On one of these vision quests, he had a remarkable experience. "It was a beautiful night," he said. "The stars were out, and it was calm—just beautiful." Around midnight he got up to pray. Then he sat for a while in the darkness. Suddenly, he began to have flashbacks—images of important and tragic moments in the history of his people and Native Americans as a whole—broken treaties, detrimental government policies, misguided missionary tactics, senseless massacres—a tragic chain of conflict and disappointment, a repetitive cycle of encroachment, retaliation, and revenge. He saw it all, one image at a time, reliving each moment as if it were fresh.

Although most of the events occurred well before he was born, the injustices were part of him. They happened to his people, and he lived in the wake of their cultural devastation. "And as I sat there I got angrier and angrier," he said, "until it turned to hatred. And I looked at the whole situation, the whole picture, and there was nothing I could do. It was too much." The only thing he *could* do, he decided, was to come off that hill, grab a gun, and start shooting—someone, anyone. If he took a path of revenge, he thought, "Maybe then my grandfathers will honor me." Against such insurmountable obstacles and grave offenses against his people, he felt powerless to do anything except strike back. But then, remarkably, he discovered another way:

> I got up. And I came around, and I faced the east. And it was beautiful. It was dawn—light—enough light to see the rolling hills out there. And right above that blue light, in that darkness, was the sliver of the moon and the morning star. And I wanted to live. I want to live. I want to be happy. I feel I deserve that. But the only way that I was going to do that was if I forgive. And I cried that morning, because I had to forgive.[1]

We often think of forgiveness as a gift we bestow on other people when they are worthy of it. And since we see our forgiveness as a gift, we sometimes withhold it as a form of punishment, but Albert White Hat learned an important truth that morning. The people and forces that tried to destroy the old Lakota ways, and consequently had been a source of so much personal pain for him, were not waiting for, nor would they benefit from, his decision to forgive. But he would.

"Since then, every day I work on that commitment," he said. And wrestling with history is something that every Lakota has to deal with. "At some point in your life, you have to address that. You have to make a decision. If you don't, you're going to die on a road someplace—either from being too drunk, or you might take a gun to your head—if you don't handle those situations."[2] Consequently, the primary benefit that Albert White Hat received by forgiving his people's oppressors was that

---

1 Albert White Hat, "One Sky Above Us," *The West*, episode 8, directed by Stephen Ives (PBS Paramount, 2004), DVD.
2 Ibid.

he liberated *himself* from their influence. When he was filled with hate, the injustices of the past dictated his response. But when he forgave, he freed himself from their debilitating effect and seized control of his own destiny. Since that turning point, he has constructively helped resist the destruction of Lakota language and culture, becoming an influential teacher and mentor. In short, he discovered and implemented one of the fundamental principles of assertive love.

Choosing Clearer Sight

Albert White Hat described forgiveness as a *decision* not an *emotion*. It is not something that comes to or acts upon us but rather is an act of will. And it can require real exertion to forgive because, as Albert White Hat noted, the past isn't really "behind" us. The past, with all its trauma, difficulty, and injustice, is "still with us" and always will be. Thus, as he observed, "we have to deal with that every day."[3] We have to regularly work on our commitment to forgive, or else the pain of the past can distract or even overwhelm us.

The ability of the past to distract and distort our lives is a dynamic I first recognized as a graduate student in Minnesota. My research focused on the national legislative and legal efforts to constrain the power of the LDS Church during the second half of the nineteenth century. Consequently, I spent many hours in the government documents section of the library, culling through congressional debates and court decisions. As I read some of the arguments against the "wicked" Mormons, often belittling or dismissing truths that I held sacred, I was often irritated by their apparent self-righteousness. How could seemingly Christian people condone or even advocate wholesale religious persecution (imprisoning hundreds of men and women, disrupting and impoverishing families, driving Church leaders into hiding) and not recognize the inconsistency and hypocrisy of their behavior? Their arguments for draconian measures such as disinheriting children, disenfranchising men and women, or confiscating Church property seemed spurious, arbitrary, and illogical. Indeed, the whole rationale for "reforming" the Church and its members made little sense to me.

One day, as I sat in the library, surrounded by piles of government publications containing seemingly endless streams of anti-Mormon rhetoric, my irritation began to escalate into anger. How could they be

---

3 Ibid.

so insensitive? How could they be so cruel? How could they not see the unnecessary pain and devastation they were causing? As I brooded over these thoughts, another quietly crept into the corner of my mind and gently pushed itself upon my consciousness. "You have to forgive them," it said, and I was startled to realize it was true. At that moment I let go, and the anger that had been rising in me suddenly dissipated, swept away by a feeling of growing peace. And for the first time in months of study, I began to understand these persecutors of my people. The logic of their actions began to make sense to me. I still didn't agree with it, but I could better understand how it made sense to them. And instead of hypocrites, I began to see well-intentioned people who were perhaps overzealous but nonetheless thought their actions would improve the world.

I realized then that I had never seen them before. Not truly. Not for who they really were. My image of these reformers had been distorted by my anger and resentment. I had coddled myself with the idea that my intentions were righteous and pure, while theirs were hypocritical and tainted. I was blind to my own hypocrisy and insensitivity. In my self-righteousness and self-serving anger, I had become blind to my own resentment, and I could not see their humanity. Once I had let go of these negative emotions that were controlling and distorting my perspective, the lives and motives of those former adversaries made greater sense to me. I discovered that day that if we really want to understand the past, we must approach it with humility, charity, and forgiveness.

Of course, all of us are historians. We are constantly culling and mentally preserving past events to help us make sense of the present. As it was with Albert White Hat, so it is with us—the past is always with us. And the way we perceive and relate to other people can be distorted if we choose to pick at old wounds and nurse old grievances. As Terry Warner has observed, only when we let go of these resentments and open ourselves to the gift of other people's humanity (even of angry and abusive people) can we see them for who they really are, and in the process liberate ourselves from the destructive control that such negative emotions wield in our lives.[4] Until I let go of my anger—my "righteous" and "well-deserved" indignation, as I preferred to think of it—I could not perceive the humanity of those nineteenth-century reformers. Their personalities, motives, and logic were enigmas I could not crack. Not until I forgave them.

4 Terry Warner, *Bonds That Make Us Free: Healing Our Relationships, Coming to Ourselves* (Salt Lake City: Shadow Mountain, 2001), 298–301.

Forgiveness = Love

Forgiveness is therefore an act of loving defiance to anger and aggression. It says, I will not hate you or strike back, but neither will I give in to your aggression. I recognize your humanity and hope to establish an equal relationship of love, respect, and trust with you. This forgiveness is the quintessential expression of the Savior's commandment to love those who are most difficult to love: "Love your enemies, bless them that curse you, do good to them that hate you, and pray for them which despitefully use you, and persecute you."[5] How can we love our enemies if we cannot forgive them? Forgiving them means loving them. And loving them means forgiving them. The two processes are inseparable and simultaneous.

But they are challenging principles to implement because they run so directly counter to our cultural training. As we have already noted, our entertainment media teaches us to root for vengeance or so-called "justice"—to take a certain satisfaction when the unrepentant bad guy "gets what's coming to him," and to feel cheated if he doesn't. Do we unwittingly transfer these entertainment attitudes to our religious beliefs? When we read our scriptures, do we experience similar satisfaction that sinners will be banished to weeping and wailing and gnashing of teeth? Do we think, "Someday, they'll get what's coming"? Or do we weep when we think of the pains they will endure?

> Forgiveness says, I will not hate you or strike back, but neither will I give in to your aggression. I recognize your humanity and hope to establish an equal relationship of love, respect, and trust with you.

The sons of Mosiah set a high standard in this regard. After their conversion they could not think of their traditional enemies in antagonistic ways. While most Nephites wanted to wage war against the Lamanites, the sons of Mosiah wanted to serve them. In other words, they felt love and forgiveness for their enemies. They were open to the gift of their humanity, and it moved them to action, "for they could not bear that any human soul should perish; yea, even the very thoughts that any soul should endure endless torment did cause them to quake and tremble."[6] Thus they were liberated from the cycle of

5 Matthew 5:44.
6 Mosiah 28:3.

conflict that infected most of Nephite society. By refusing to be offended or resentful, they refused their consent to allow those emotions power in their lives.

Who, then, are our enemies? Most can be grouped into two broad categories—*distant* and *near*. Distant enemies are easy to hate and hard to love because we do not personally know them. If we keep them remote, it is easier to demonize them. Unfortunately, this dynamic has been exacerbated by technology. Internet communication can often spawn astonishingly cruel and spiteful comments because the human connection is so distant. People are so physically and emotionally separated that they can no longer perceive one another's humanity, thus they find it easier to say hateful things. But whether we voice our sentiments or not, all of us probably have some distant enemies that we find easy to demonize. Whether they be international terrorists, pornographers, members of another political party, fans of a rival sports team, or an annoying celebrity, we find it easy to hate and difficult to love and forgive these distant, impersonal "enemies."

But while it is difficult to forgive our distant enemies, sometimes it's even harder to forgive those who are nearest to us—family members, neighbors, and friends who injure us in the most intimate ways. A business associate who cheats us. A customer who unfairly yells at us. A family member or friend who betrays our trust. How can we possibly love and forgive those who curse, hate, or despitefully use us—and not from a distance but in a very close and personal manner? This is especially difficult if they seem unrepentant.

But forgiveness *is* possible. We simply have to choose to open ourselves to the humanity of our enemies—both near and distant. As always, God provides the most poignant example. When Jesus cried, "Father, forgive them; for they know not what they do," He demonstrated a remarkable compassion and recognition of the humanity of His oppressors.[7] But His sincere love was not the only, or even the most impressive, example of forgiveness that day. His cry also implied an even more extraordinary example of love and forgiveness from His Father. Anyone who has watched a loved one being hurt knows it is often easier to absorb pain into ourselves than to watch it inflicted on someone else. Likewise, it is often easier to forgive someone who injures us than to forgive someone who injures a person we love. It must have

---

7 Luke 23:34.

been overwhelming for the Father, even as perfect and fully developed as His love was, to watch His Only Begotten Son dying at the cruel hands of some of His less faithful children. Perhaps Jesus sensed His Father's anguish and so cried out for Him to forgive the tormentors, thus bolstering His Father's perfect love in this moment of excruciating pain.

So how about us? Can we forgive that politician? That terrorist? That pornographer? Can we forgive that cheating business associate? That rude customer? That false and fickle family member? Even and especially if they are unrepentant? Forgiveness, even in the most difficult circumstances, is the Balm of Gilead. And the paradox of its power is that while forgiveness may or may not be received by the people toward whom it is directed, it is always soothing for the person in whose heart it resides. It gently washes the soul of enmity and wraps the heart in peace and goodwill. In the end, forgiveness heals and liberates *us* more that it heals and liberates *them* because when we choose to exert forgiveness, the destructive elements of that relationship no longer have influence in our lives.

This is why forgiveness—true, compassionate, selfless forgiveness—is an act of loving defiance to anger and aggression. Whether or not the other people we forgive accept our choice, we have changed the dynamic by which we relate to them. Forgiveness shatters cycles of conflict and deprives our "enemies" of the fuel they need to justify their anger and aggression. A sixteenth-century French philosopher noted that the oppressors in our lives are only as powerful as we choose to make them, and when we surrender to their abuse we only fuel their influence:

Everyone knows that the fire from a little spark will increase and blaze ever higher as long as it finds wood to burn; yet without being quenched by water, but merely by finding no more fuel to feed on, it consumes itself, dies down, and is no longer a flame. Similarly, the more tyrants pillage, the more they crave, the more they ruin and destroy; the more one yields to them, and obeys them, by that much do they become mightier and more formidable, the readier to annihilate and destroy. But if not one thing is yielded to them, if, without any violence they are simply not obeyed, they become naked and undone and as nothing, just as, when the root receives no nourishment, the branch withers and dies.[8]

8 Étienne de la Boétie, *The Politics of Obedience: The Discourse of Voluntary Servitude*, trans. Harry Kurz (Montreal: Black Rose Books, 1997), 50–51.

Comprehensive and compassionate forgiveness starves a conflict of its essential fuel. In the best of circumstances, once our enemies shoulder the entire burden of anger, once we no longer help to fuel or justify their aggression, they can rediscover that humanity. Then they may feel the injustice of their behavior and choose to repent. This is what happened to the Lamanites who slaughtered the people of Ammon:

Forgiveness shatters cycles of conflict and deprives our "enemies" of the fuel they need to justify their anger and aggression.

starved of the violent defense they expected, the Lamanite oppressors were left naked and exposed in their own unjust aggression. They were "stung" by their murderous behavior and their hearts were "swollen." They rediscovered their humanity, and they threw themselves on the ground in solidarity with people who had been their enemies only moments earlier.

This is the best of all possible responses. But even if our enemies (either near or distant) are not touched by our forgiveness, even if they continue to rant and rail and abuse, our forgiveness changes the dynamic. And confronted with such assertive love, our enemies can no longer exert power in our lives (unless, of course, they choose to repent and rebuild their influence on righteous principles of love and trust). It may well be that when unrepentant enemies sense their influence is diminishing that they will *escalate* their negative behavior rather than decrease it, at least for a time. This only represents a flailing attempt to hold onto a power that is slipping away, such as Satan ranting at Moses when the fledgling prophet would not bow down and worship him.[9] But if we hold true to our love and forgiveness, as Moses held true to his convictions, our unrepentant enemies will discover, as Satan did, that they have no influence—that they cannot shake our assertive love for them.

Forgiveness ≠ Trust

As I have pondered these principles and grappled with implementing them in my own life, I have asked a question that perhaps comes to your mind as well—if we love and forgive those who hurt us, especially those who don't change their behavior, must we continue to absorb their violence? Must we continue to endure scorn and contempt from abusive

9 Moses 1:12–22.

spouses? Must we continue to work for tyrants? Must we retain close ties with friends who are selfish or manipulative? Every situation is unique, but it is helpful to remember that although *forgiveness* is a form of assertive love, trust is fundamentally different.

My first mission president tried to teach me this principle, but it took me years to appreciate the lesson: As a young missionary, I craved the approval of that mission president, an imposing but gentle man, a gospel scholar with seemingly infinite knowledge and wisdom. When he came into a room, he would wrap his arms around some of the missionaries, pulling them close in a giant hug. When he conducted interviews with missionaries, I envied the long lazy time he seemed to spend with some of them, while my encounters seemed distressingly brief. Perhaps he sensed my longing and dissatisfaction because once, sitting in the dim light of our apartment, near the end of one of our compact interviews, he paused, took my hand, and looked me in the eye. "I want you to know I trust you," he said. "And trust is better than love."

No, it's not, I thought as he left our apartment and drove off into the night, *love is the greatest of all*. And I still craved that love—or what I mistakenly took as the tokens of his love—more than his trust. Although I was a stubborn student, I sensed, even at the time, that he meant to give me a great compliment. It wasn't until years later that the significance of that compliment (and the meaning of his long interviews with others) began to seep in. Similar to God, my mission president loved everyone. But he couldn't necessarily trust all his missionaries, and some required more attention, more frequent and extended expressions of his love. He loved me, and deep down I knew and felt his love, despite our brief encounters. What he was trying to teach me was that his *love* was free, regardless of my behavior. *Trust*, on the other hand, has to be earned. And he wanted me to know I had earned his.

That is the fundamental difference between love and trust, and since forgiveness is a form of love, it is also the fundamental difference between forgiveness and trust. They are not the same, though we often mistake them as interchangeable. Consequently, although the Lord frequently encourages us to love everyone (including our enemies) and forgive everyone (including the unrepentant), He cautions us about where and in whom to place our trust. Trust is something that is earned. We should be open, willing, and even eager to trust other people, and we should look for every opportunity to allow others, even those who have broken our trust, to prove their trustworthiness. But there is no *requirement* to trust, and sometimes when trust has been violated severely enough, we may even have to sever a relationship. But such steps are drastic and should only be taken with the greatest care and reluctance because severing relationships is a form of violence. This attitude of the Nephites as they went to battle against the Lamanites provides a good model:

> Now, they were sorry to take up arms against the Lamanites, because they did not delight in the shedding of blood; yea, and this was not all—they were sorry to be the means of sending so many of their brethren out of this world into an eternal world, unprepared to meet their God. Nevertheless, they could not suffer to lay down their lives, that their wives and their children should be massacred by the barbarous cruelty of those who were once their brethren.[10]

We must choose to love those who injure us—to forgive them and pray for their happiness and success—but in extreme cases we may also have to guard against them. Even the people of Ammon, who wielded love and exerted forgiveness with remarkable success, eventually sought sanctuary among the Nephites. Some of their enemies were so callous, so indifferent to their own humanity and the humanity of those they hated that if the people of Ammon had not fled to the protection of the Nephites, they would have been utterly destroyed.

Nevertheless, we must avoid the temptation to rush to such judgments. Too often we can use this logic to justify our own indifference, callousness, or selfish desires. While it may sometimes be necessary to defend ourselves against our enemies (far and near), the spirit in which we enact these defenses is crucial. We must be as the Nephites, filled with love and forgiveness, coming to our defensive violence (resorting to the lesser law) only with "much reluctance."[11]

Possible & Practical

Is such assertive love and forgiveness really possible? Yes. As children of God, we have that divine capacity within us. At times it may feel beyond us, but if we simply choose the path of forgiveness, God will meet us there—and assist us. The Atonement of Christ allows you and me an opportunity to lean on God's assertive love when we cannot fully muster

---

10 Alma 48:23–24.
11 Alma 48:22.

our own. His perfect, complete, fully developed love and forgiveness are gifts for which we can ask, and which He promises to grant. The prophet Mormon implored us to "pray unto the Father with all the energy of heart, that ye may be filled with this love."[12] One of the most dramatic examples of this principle was famously described by Corrie ten Boom, a Dutch Christian who helped many Jews escape and who was later imprisoned by the Nazis for her efforts. A few years after the war, she gave a speech in a Munich church about forgiveness and the power of God. After her speech, "a balding, heavyset man in a gray overcoat" approached her. He had been a guard at the camp where she and her older sister had been held and where her sister had died.

It came back with a rush: the huge room with its harsh overhead lights, the pathetic pile of dresses and shoes in the center of the floor, the shame of walking naked past this man. I could see my sister's frail form ahead of me, ribs sharp beneath the parchment of skin. . . .

Now he was in front of me, hand thrust out: "A fine message, fraulein! How good it is to know that, as you say, all our sins are at the bottom of the sea!"

And I, who had spoken so glibly of forgiveness, fumbled in my pocketbook rather than take his hand. . . .

I was face to face with one of my captors and my blood seemed to freeze.

"You mentioned Ravensbruck in your talk," he was saying. "I was a guard there. . . . But since that time," he went on, "I have become a Christian. I know that God has forgiven me for the cruel things I did there, but I would like to hear it from your lips as well. Fraulein"—again the hand came out—"will you forgive me?"

And I stood there—I whose sins had again and again been forgiven—and could not forgive. Betsie had died in that place—could he erase her slow terrible death simply for the asking? . . .

But forgiveness is not an emotion—I knew that too. Forgiveness is an act of the will, and the will can function regardless of the temperature of the heart. "Jesus, help me!" I prayed silently. "I can lift my hand. I can do that much. You supply the feeling."

And so woodenly, mechanically, I thrust my hand into the one stretched out to me. And as I did, an incredible thing took place.

12 Moroni 7:48.

The current started in my shoulder, raced down my arm, sprang into our joined hands. And then this healing warmth seemed to flood my whole being, bringing tears to my eyes.

"I forgive you, brother!" I cried. "With all my heart!"

For a long moment we grasped each other's hands, the former guard and former prisoner. I had never known God's love so intensely as I did then.[13]

Just as Mormon had promised, when Corrie ten Boom prayed "with all the energy of heart," she was "filled with this love." When she exerted the act of will to forgive—stepping onto the path, even mechanically—she discovered she had the capacity to do something she thought was beyond her.

Anytime we exert our will to love and forgive, the love of God can work in our hearts. That liberates us—not from our relationships themselves but from their destructive effects of anger and aggression. Such love can also work miracles in the hearts of our adversaries. Stanley Peterson, a former administrator with the Church Education System, discovered this truth as a young educator. When he was only twenty-seven, he was hired as the principal of an elementary school. Most of the teachers seemed willing to give this young administrator the benefit of the doubt, but the only male teacher, a older man named Al, was hostile from the beginning. He'd been teaching at the school for over twenty years and had expected to be made its principal. Consequently, he saw Stan's appointment as an insult and a threat. The young principal tried his best to be Al's friend, but the older teacher rebuffed him and did everything he could to make life miserable. Stan began having nightmares: "I remember one night I dreamed we were having a faculty meeting and Al and I got into a fight and were rolling around on the floor while the lady teachers all stood around screaming."

The crisis came to a head when Stan filled out teacher evaluations at the end of the year. He was required to rate each teacher in several categories according to three options: 1) Above District Standards, 2) Meets District Standards, or 3) Below District Standards. The following category gave him pause: "Rate this individual's ability to relate well with fellow teachers." As Stan described it, Al had constant confrontations with other

---

13 Corrie ten Boom, *Tramp for the Lord*, with Jamie Buckingham (New York: Jove Books, 1978), 53–55.

teachers: "To rate Al at any level but below district standards would have been a lie so I bit the bullet and rated him accordingly." Predictably, when Al met with Stan and was handed the evaluation, he exploded:

He stood over me and began to shout obscenities. . . . He began by attacking the university I attended, BYU–Provo, my church, my family, my youthful age, my philosophy of teaching, etc. etc. etc. To be honest with you, I was amazed at how much he knew about me. For about fifteen minutes he screamed every filthy, negative and cutting remark about everything he thought would be hurtful to me. I'm sure he had rehearsed in his mind that speech for months and had waited for the right time to launch it.

Then he just stopped, and the room was silent. For one thing, I think he was exhausted from screaming at the top of his voice for so long and for another thing, I think he now wanted me to give a response so he could give his rebuttal to whatever I might fire back at him.

I have to confess that there were many things that went through my mind that I would have liked to say in response, but none of them would have been appropriate. . . . So for about two minutes I sat silently saying a mental prayer that I would be guided to give the appropriate response.

Finally I broke the long silence, and in a very quiet voice I said, "Al, whatever I have done to you to make you hate me so badly, I apologize to you for offending you. I am very sorry. But I want you to know something, I love you as my brother and I would like to be your friend." Then I said nothing more.

The room was very quiet. I think Al was ready for almost any response I might have given except for "I'm sorry if I have offended you, I love you, and I want to be your friend."

We sat in silence for a few minutes, and then Al did something I wasn't prepared for. He began to cry. He finally gained his composure and said these few words. "No one has ever told me they loved me in my entire life. Not even my mother or father," and with that he left the room.

In the months that followed, Al and I became good friends and when I left that school to take another assignment, Al came up to me, put his arms around me, and began to cry. Finally he said, "I don't want you to leave, you are the best friend I have ever had."[14]

Stan's conscious act to exert forgiveness, his willingness to be open to the gift of Al's humanity, invited the love of God and exposed Al's violence as unjustified and ineffective. Al, in turn, responded to Stan's surprising decision and the divine love it invited by choosing to open himself to the gift of Stan's humanity.

Not all examples are so dramatic or immediate. But hopefully all of us can remember subtler moments when we chose to forgive, regardless of the merits of the person, and the freedom and peace that such choices naturally brought. We can choose to forgive a cutting remark, a betrayal, a disappointment, a deceitful action. When we do, we find that we see our offenders in a whole new light. Before, we were focused inward, at our own challenges, our discomfort, our pain, but forgiveness spreads and enlarges our souls. The scales fall from our eyes, and we recognize their challenges, their discomfort, their pain. We are thus liberated from our hurt because we have allowed ourselves to perceive and care about their humanity. But it is even more than that. Since we are all children of God, what we are responding to is probably not their humanity but something deeper. We are open for the first time to the reality of their *divinity*.

---

14 Stanley A. Peterson, "Contention Is Not of Me," devotional address delivered at Brigham Young University–Idaho, 14 October 2003.

Chapter 6
REAWAKENING OUR AFFILIATIONS

ONE OF MY DEEPEST AND most irrational fears is that someone will break into my home and harm my family. I live in a safe and tranquil neighborhood with one of the lowest violent crime rates in the country. But each night, before I retire, I check and double-check the bolts on the doors. Even then, I occasionally wake in the middle of the night, sure I heard someone moving downstairs. Sometimes I even go through the house, opening every closet, peering into every corner and behind every piece of furniture, just to be sure the house is empty of intruders. It is a childish fear, I know. But in other ways, it is simply fatherly—I worry about protecting my wife and children. What would I do if they were threatened? How might I shield them from harm? Would a weapon of love work under such extreme and immediate circumstances? Or would a gun be more effective? I hope I never have to find out. I hope I never have to go through such an ordeal.

But Angie O'Gorman did. She woke one night to the sound of a man, a complete stranger, kicking in her bedroom door. "The house was empty. The phone was downstairs. He was somewhat verbally abusive as he walked over to my bed. I could not find his eyes in the darkness but could see the outline of his form." In that terrifying moment, as Angie experienced "a fear and vulnerability I had never before experienced," several thoughts rushed through her mind. The first was that screaming would be useless. The second was that even if she'd had a gun, she had no time to reach for it. But it was the third thought—an unexpected and surprising one—that she believed saved her life:

> I realized with a certain clarity that either he and I made it through this situation safely—together—or we would be both damaged. Our safety was connected. If he raped me, I would be hurt

both physically and emotionally. If he raped me, he would be hurt as well. If he went to prison, the damage would be greater. That thought disarmed *me*. It freed me from my own desire to lash out and at the same time from my own paralysis. It did not free me from feelings of fear but from fear's control over my ability to respond.[1]

This was the pivotal moment, when she recognized that both her safety and the safety of her violent intruder were linked together. Once she realized this simple truth, fear no longer controlled her response. She could see and react with a clarity that fear usually masks: "I found myself acting out of concern for both our safety which caused me to react with a certain firmness but with surprisingly little hostility in my voice." And her reaction to his aggression was unusual, to say the least:

I asked him what time it was. He answered. That was a good sign. I commented that his watch and the clock on my night table had different times. His said 2:30; mine said 2:45. I had just set mine. I hoped his watch wasn't broken. When had he last set it? He answered. I answered. The time seemed endless. When the atmosphere began to calm a little I asked him how he had gotten into the house. He'd broken through the glass in the back door. I told him that presented me with a problem as I did not have the money to buy new glass. He talked about some financial difficulties of his own. We talked until we were no longer strangers and I felt it was safe to ask him to leave. He didn't want to, said he had no place to go. Knowing I did not have the physical power to force him out I told him firmly but respectfully, as equal to equal, I would give him a clean set of sheets, but he would have to make his own bed downstairs. He went downstairs, and I sat up in bed wide awake and shaking for the rest of the night. The next morning we ate breakfast together, and he left.[2]

While this experience is extraordinary on several levels, it highlights a simple truth. When Angie O'Gorman realized that this stranger's life was interconnected with hers, she became liberated from her own potential anger and fear-induced aggression, and her subsequent behavior changed the whole dynamic:

1 Angie O'Gorman, "Defense through Disarmament: Nonviolence and Personal Assault," in *The Universe Bends Toward Justice*, ed. Angie O'Gorman (Philadelphia: New Society Publishers, 1990), 242–243.
2 Ibid., 243.

Several things happened that night. I allowed someone who I was afraid of to become human to me, and as a result I reacted in a surprisingly human way to him. That caught him off guard. Apparently his scenario had not included a social visit, and it took him a few minutes to regain his sense of balance. By that time the vibes were all wrong for violence. Whatever had been motivating him was sidetracked, and he changed his mind.[3]

The man probably expected one of two responses to his intrusion— she would either cower in fear or violently resist him. What he did not expect was for her to treat him with calm humanity, to engage him in an "equal-to-equal" conversation as she would a friend or relative. It was her sense of connection to him that allowed her to respond this way, with firm but loving resistance. Her response invited—in fact, almost *required*—him to respond to her in an equally human way. And once an emotional connection had been forged, "the vibes were all wrong for violence." With a mutually recognized connection, he could no more do violence to her than he could to himself because now she was part of him. And it all began with one simple but liberating thought—*our lives are connected.*

Spiritual & Physical Affiliations

Many languages include common greetings of peace and goodwill. The Hebrew word "shalom" is a literal greeting of "peace." Muslims hail others with "asalam alaykum," which means "peace be upon you." Hawaiians have their ubiquitous and touching "Aloha," with its wonderful connotations of love, compassion, and mercy. But one of my favorite greetings comes from India and its Hindu traditions. People salute each other by bowing slightly, with their palms pressed together like hands in prayer. "Namaste," they say, which means, "the divine in me bows to the divine in you."

All of us are divine. All of us are children of the same God. All of us, including our enemies, are brothers and sisters. And we "bow" to each other because our lives and fates are interconnected. We were connected in the premortal world, and we are connected here. What Joseph Smith taught concerning our ancestors applies to the entire human race—"we without them cannot be made perfect; neither can they without us be made perfect."[4]

---

3 Ibid.
4 Doctrine and Covenants 128:18.

This interconnectedness is not simply a mystical or spiritual theory but rather a physiological fact. Scientists call these relationships *limbic resonance* and *limbic regulation*, referring to the limbic lobe in the brain, a feature common to all mammals but especially well developed in humans. It is the limbic lobe that interprets subtle emotional cues that all people give through their hands, posture, eyes, skin, and voice. Limbic resonance is therefore a "symphony of mutual exchange and internal adaptation whereby two [people] become attuned to each other's inner states."[5] Thus limbic regulation is the process by which two people establish a circle of influence, literally regulating each other's physiological rhythms.

The human body constantly fine-tunes many thousands of physiologic parameters—heart rate and blood pressure, body temperature, immune functions, oxygen saturation, levels of sugars, hormones, salts, ions, metabolites. In a closed-loop design, each body would self-monitor levels and self-administer correctives, keeping its solitary system in continuous harmonious balance.

But because human physiology is (at least in part) an open-loop arrangement, an individual does not direct all of his own functions. A second person transmits regulatory information that can alter hormone levels, cardiovascular function, sleep rhythms, immune function, and more—inside the body of the first. The reciprocal process occurs simultaneously: the first person regulates the physiology of the second, even as he himself is regulated. Neither is a functioning whole on his own; each has open loops that only somebody else can complete.[6]

We literally *cannot live* without each other. This fact was tragically demonstrated nearly eight hundred years ago, when Frederick II, a Holy Roman emperor, tried to determine the inborn language of humans—the "original tongue"—by denying newborn infants any social interaction. They were amply fed, clothed, and cleaned, but nothing else. All of the infants died before speaking a word. Similar results from orphanages in the 1940s likewise demonstrated what scientists have now confirmed: "a lack of human interaction—handling, cooing, stroking, baby talk, and

---

5 Thomas Lewis, Fari Amini, and Richard Lannon, *A General Theory of Love* (New York: Vintage Books, 2000), 63.
6 Ibid., 85.

play—is fatal to infants."[7] Adults are better at living in isolation but not much. Our lives are interconnected—literally.

While those with whom we form the most intimate emotional bonds clearly have the greatest physiological influence in our lives, the processes of limbic resonance and regulation mean the entire human race is ultimately interconnected. Although we may at times feel isolated and independent, we cannot be. My emotions ripple physiologically through and beyond other people in my life. No matter how small my circle of influence may seem, those people I touch, those lives with which I have the most intense resonance and regulation, are connected to others, and they to others still, until the entire human family is linked through a vast reverberating web. A tremor from a distant corner of that web may eventually shake my own. And I, in turn, may send waves to places I cannot imagine. Consequently, as children of God, our lives and futures are linked together—not just spiritually but physiologically as well. This simple but elegant truth was eloquently expressed by the Native American poet Manitongquat:

> Life is the Sacred Mystery singing to itself,
> dancing to its drum, telling tales, improving, playing
> and we all that Spirit,
> our stories all but one cosmic story
> that we are love indeed,
> that perfect love in me seeks the love in you,
> and if our eyes could ever meet without fear
> we would recognize each other and rejoice,
> for love is life believing in itself.[8]

Straining & Severing

Even after we comprehend that all of our lives and fates are connected, we too often forget this fact when it counts most—when anger, fear, greed, or lust wells within our hearts. But divine affiliations are crucial because violence is only possible when they become strained,

---

7 Ibid., 68–70.
8 As quoted in Sir John Templeton, *Agape Love: A Tradition Found in Eight World Religions* (Philadelphia: Templeton Foundation Press, 1999), 6.

stretched, or severed. The farther we are from someone else—physically, culturally, spiritually, or emotionally—the easier it is to inflict violence on them. Political and military leaders understand this. Propaganda that dehumanizes the enemy is a crucial part of any war. And long-distance combat, which is facilitated by increasing advances in technology, makes war less personal, both physically and psychologically. The closer a soldier is to his "target" (either spatially or emotionally), the more time he has to think about the possible similarities or connections he might share with that enemy and the less inclined he is to pull the trigger.

The Allies and the Central powers learned this lesson during the First World War. After hostilities broke out in the summer of 1914, the war quickly stalemated with deeply entrenched positions along the western front. Both sides employed massive propaganda machines to demonize the other and bolster their soldiers' resolve to fight. But then a curious thing happened. On Christmas Eve, in many locations along the lines, a spontaneous truce erupted. In some places it began with German soldiers lighting candles on small Christmas trees. In others, voices began serenading the opposing trenches with carols. Soon, men emerged from the trenches and met each other in the "no man's land" between the barbed wire. They exchanged food, gifts, letters. They played soccer. In some places they staged impromptu concerts and performances for each other.[9] For a brief moment—and in some places it lasted for several days—formerly fierce enemies established or rediscovered their divine connectedness. They became open to each other's gifts of humanity.

As you can imagine, this had an effect on their capacity to perpetuate violence. For several days afterwards, German soldiers in one unit went on strike, refusing to shoot at their enemies, no matter how much the officers encouraged them. "We can't," the soldiers said, "they are good fellows, and we can't." Having established divine connections, the men did not wish to sever them again. Finally, under threat of a firing squad, the German soldiers agreed to fire their weapons. But, as one soldier recalled, they fired them only in the air: "We spent that day and the next . . . wasting ammunition in trying to shoot the stars down from the sky."[10] Many Allied soldiers and officers showed a similar reluctance to resume the violence.

---

9 See Stanley Weintraub, *Silent Night: The Story of the World War I Christmas Truce* (New York: Free Press, 2001). The French film *Joyeux Noël* (2005) also provides a beautiful and touching characterization of the truce.

10 As quoted in Weintraub, *Silent Night*, 141.

Recognizing that such personal connections would spoil the rampant anger and aggression that was necessary to continue the conflict, one British general observed, "I have issued the strictest orders that on no account is intercourse to be allowed between the opposing troops. To finish this war quickly, we must keep up the fighting spirit and do all we can to discourage friendly intercourse." Orders on the German side were similar—*Die Schützengrabenfreundschaft verboten* (friendship between the trenches forbidden).[11]

To maintain the war, the generals and politicians had to maintain a "proper" distance between their soldiers and the enemy. Friendliness might reawaken divine connections, which might lead in turn to another spontaneous peace—ironically enough, the last thing political leaders on either side really wanted, sitting as they were in their capital cities, far from the front lines and the carnage. And over the next weeks and months, as the violence gradually increased and anger and a vengeful spirit returned, the divine connection that had been established between the soldiers on the front lines was again stretched and finally severed. So the violence continued for nearly four years.

It is easy to decry the senseless tragedy of the First World War—a generation of young men slaughtered because of their leaders' pettiness and pride. Such carnage evokes an image, as Enoch once saw, of God weeping from his heavens because his children, so full of divine potential and relatedness "are without affection, and they hate their own blood."[12] Yet we too often do similar things in our relationships. Too often we are "without affection" for our "enemies"—bosses, neighbors, friends, family members. We wage quiet but equally destructive wars against them because we forget, as do most soldiers, our divine affiliations and interdependency. We employ intimate forms of propaganda (more commonly known as "gossip") to bolster our pride and downplay their divinity. And we create distance (sometimes physical but more often emotional) to stretch and ultimately sever the divine connections that would lovingly bind us to each other.

Technology makes this process easier. Although it helps bridge the challenge of physical distance, the Internet can also exacerbate emotional distance. Perusing online discussions such as the "comments" section of a news article or a blog provides quick evidence of how seldom divine connections are facilitated by that environment. Wrapped within the

---

11 Ibid., 148 and 151.
12 Moses 7:28–33.

supposed "safety" of anonymity, isolated in their homes or offices, people feel free to criticize, demonize, and even violently abuse people in ways they never would consider if they saw those people face-to-face. This is because limbic resonance, the ability to discern another person's inner state, can only work effectively in a face-to-face environment, where subtle emotional cues can be adequately discerned. Emoticons (textual symbols intended to convey emotions) have tried to correct this handicap of online communication, but no matter how complex or witty an emoticon may be, it can never replace the complexity of another person's voice, touch, or countenance. We cannot look into another person's countenance—really look, with openness and charity—without realizing their astonishing capacity, without somehow becoming lost in the gift of their divinity. As C. S. Lewis noted:

> It is in the light of these overwhelming possibilities, it is with the awe and circumspection proper to them, that we should conduct all our dealings with one another, all friendships, all loves, all play, all politics. There are no ordinary people. You have never talked to a mere mortal. Nations, cultures, arts, civilizations—these are mortal and their life is to ours as the life of a gnat. But it is immortals whom we joke with, work with, marry, snub, and exploit.[13]

Most of what we need to develop as socially healthy human beings comes from connection, but some experts in the science of emotion fear that our modern world, saturated as it is with entertainment but increasingly empty of meaningful human connection, may be producing children with "limbic deficits." And "a limbically damaged human is deadly," these experts note, because the brain's "intricate, interlocking neural barriers to violence" will not be in place to restrain behavior. The spark of healthy human connectedness lies within all of us, but "if we do not shelter that spark, guide and nurture it, then we not only lose the life within but we unleash later destruction upon ourselves."[14] Then, as with the First World War, violence may become endemic. People will live "without affection." And whole generations may be lost.

Reconnecting

Breaking cycles of conflict means reestablishing our spiritual and temporal connections. Assertive love works in part by reawakening our

---

13 C. S. Lewis, *The Weight of Glory and Other Addresses* (San Francisco: HarperCollins, 2001), 46.

14 Lewis, Amini, and Lannon, *A General Theory of Love*, 217–219.

affinities—our spontaneous and natural sympathies—and inviting those with whom we are in conflict to do the same. This is what happened to Angie O'Gorman. First she realized the way in which her life and the life of the stranger were linked. With that thought she was liberated from the violence of typical responses and became open to his humanity. Realizing that her fate was connected to his, she was able to feel genuine concern for his welfare, and her response was both startling and humane, inviting him to see the connection as well.

Each time assertive love has been effectively employed against anger and aggression, the person wielding it has found a way to emphasize interconnectedness through an unexpected act of humanity. Ammon, for example, offered to live among and serve his traditional enemies. Angie O'Gorman asked her assailant for the time. There is no magic formula only a pattern of demonstrating interdependence, cultivating what Angie O'Gorman calls a "context of conversion," which invites the other person to respond in kind.[15]

Dallin H. Oaks experienced this pattern during a harrowing incident in 1970 when he was a law professor at the University of Chicago. His wife, June, had been attending a Church leadership meeting one night, and he came to drive her home. Another sister needed a ride to her apartment, which was located in a gang-infested neighborhood. Having lived several years in the area, Dallin and June Oaks took certain precautions. She remained in the car with the keys in the ignition in case she needed to drive away, as he walked the other sister to her apartment door. Returning to the lobby, he surveyed the street and observed that it was empty except for three young men. He waited until they were out of sight before stepping out of the building and into the street. But as he reached the car, and just as June was reaching across to unlock the door, one of the young men came running back, brandishing a gun. There was no time to get in the car, and fortunately, June saw the approaching threat and wisely left the door locked. Then, as she watched in horror, the young man thrust the barrel of the gun into her husband's stomach and demanded money.

Dallin Oaks took his wallet out of his pocket and showed the young robber that it was empty. "Give me your car keys," the young man demanded. When he was told they were in the car, the young man demanded that June open the door. When this request was denied, the

15 O'Gorman, *The Universe Bends Towards Justice*, 243.

young man became furious, pushing the gun into his victim's stomach and saying, "Do it, or I'll kill you." When Dallin Oaks again refused, the young robber repeated his demands with an even angrier tone and greater movement with his gun. Elder Oaks recalled, "I remember thinking that he probably wouldn't shoot me on purpose, but if he wasn't careful in the way he kept jabbing that gun into my stomach, he might shoot me by mistake. His gun looked like a cheap one, and I was nervous about its firing mechanism."

The stalemate continued for what felt as an eternity, as June watched helplessly from inside the car. "Give me your money." "I don't have any." "Give me your car keys." "They're in the car." "Tell her to open the car." "I won't do it." "I'll kill you if you don't." "I won't do it." Finally, a city bus approached. It stopped close to the two men, and a passenger got off. But even though the driver looked directly at them, he was obviously not inclined to intervene, and he began driving on. This happened behind the young robber, out of his view, and the unseen activity made him anxious and distracted so that he lowered his gun a little. Dallin Oaks saw an opportunity. If he acted quickly, he could grab the gun. He was bigger than the young man and was convinced he could overpower him in a one-on-one struggle, thus disabling the threat.

Up to this point, the possible responses that Dallin Oaks considered were typically dichotomous—either give in by unlocking the door or strike back by seizing the gun. But then he had a divine insight that completely transformed the dynamic: "Just as I was about to make my move, I had a unique experience. I did not see anything or hear anything, but I *knew* something. I knew what would happen if I grabbed that gun. We would struggle, and I would turn the gun into that young man's chest. It would fire, and he would die. I also understood that I must not have the blood of that young man on my conscience for the rest of my life."

In a moment remarkably similar to the one Angie O'Gorman experienced, Dallin Oaks became aware of the link between his fate and the fate of the young man. If he tried to seize the gun, both of them would be harmed. And, just as it did for Angie O'Gorman, this thought liberated him and opened up new avenues of activity: "I relaxed, and as the bus pulled away I followed an impulse to put my right hand on his shoulder and give him a lecture. June and I had some teenage children at that time, and giving lectures came naturally. 'Look here,' I said. 'This isn't right. What you're doing just isn't right. The next car might be a policeman, and you could get killed or sent to jail for this.'"[16]

The gentle touch of a hand along with a surprisingly kind and fatherly concern threw off the whole dynamic. Having opened himself to the humanity of this young man and having established both an emotional and physical connection, Dallin Oaks subtly invited the young man to receive the gift of his humanity, recognize their divine connection, and consider a different course of action. His genuine interest in the young man, born out of this connection and made tangible by his touch, emotionally disarmed the robber. After that, to borrow Angie O'Gorman's words, "the vibes were all wrong for violence."

"With the gun back in my stomach, the young robber replied to my lecture by going through his demands for the third time. But this time his voice was subdued. When he offered the final threat to kill me, he didn't sound persuasive. When I refused again, he hesitated for a moment and then stuck the gun in his pocket and ran away."[17] Confronted with a physical, emotional, and spiritual connection, the robber fled. The young man's response was perhaps less sociable than Angie O'Gorman's attacker's had been; nevertheless, the dynamic had been fundamentally altered. Violence had become less tenable for the would-be assailant. He could still hurt this man who had expressed genuine concern for him. The young man now had very little justification for such a cold-blooded act, so he chose to leave.

This is a fundamental key to weapons of love—closing the distances that facilitate violence. By reawakening and reasserting our divine affiliations, our shared fate, we draw closer to those with whom we are in conflict, making violence increasingly difficult for them to justify. Of course, we cannot guarantee that other people will respond, that they will accept the gift of our humanity. The people of Ammon, after all, reawakened a sense of divine connection in *most* but not *all* of their enemies. For some, the Nephite apostates in particular, their anger had grown so intense that they were "past feeling." A weapon of love carries no guarantees. There are risks. But no weapon is failsafe, and a weapon of love is more effective than other alternatives. The practical advantage of assertive love is that by closing the distance rather than augmenting it

---

16 Dallin H. Oaks, "Bible Stories and Personal Protection," *Ensign* (November 1992).
17 Ibid.

by giving in or striking back, assertive love makes a violent response *less* probable rather than more.

The best we can do is create what Angie O'Gorman called a "context of conversion." Dallin Oaks did this by placing his hand on the young robber's shoulder and lecturing him as a father would. But the connection doesn't have to be physical or even visual. My sister remembers a night, when she was a teenager, that she and my mother had a massive blow-up. Holly left the house fuming, fleeing to a friend's home to nurse her wounds. Later that night, when she thought our mother wouldn't notice, she snuck back into the house and up to her room, where she locked the door and climbed on her bed, her anger from the explosive encounter, now hours old, still seething within her.

There was a knock on her door.

She didn't answer.

Then, through the door, my mother's voice bridged the distance. "Holly, I just want you to know I love you."

With that, Holly's anger suddenly drained away, and she began to cry.

What made this brief encounter so effective? It wasn't necessarily the words, although the message they conveyed was certainly important. Rather, it was something deeper. The timbre of our mother's voice created a connection; it conveyed sincere concern for Holly and offered an invitation to reciprocate. Such sincerity cannot be feigned. Our limbic brains, so finely tuned to emotional cues, can quickly detect false sympathy, forced affiliation, or other motives. My mother could not have disarmed my sister without a genuine sense of their fundamental interdependence.

> **The practical advantage of assertive love is that by closing the distance . . . assertive love makes a violent response less probable.**

And that reality was transmitted without effort or even consciousness through Holly's door.

Perhaps our divine connections are more easily remembered in our families, within which we have a natural sense of relatedness. But even then, when we experience conflict, as we inevitably do, we can too easily forget how intimately and thoroughly our fates—our shared safety—are linked. Paradoxically, it is often that closeness that makes reconnection difficult. Those closest to us can often cause us the greatest pain and thus create the most poignant alienations, but when divine affiliations are reawakened, such reunions become all the sweeter. Consequently, when conflicts emerge outside our families and close friends, the process often requires greater concentration because we don't naturally sense our affiliations. The more distant others are from us (physically, culturally, ideologically), the harder it is to remember and reestablish those divine connections.

But regardless of whether we are trying to reawaken our affinities with intimate relations or distant enemies, the pattern is the same. There is no sure recipe to always evoke this divine connectedness. Such moments of awakening seem almost serendipitous—unexpected gifts from a loving Father. But we can prepare ourselves to receive them. Angie O'Gorman attributed her unusual sense of connection and her response to "the effects of prayer, meditation, training and the experience of lesser kinds of assault." So when a would-be rapist crashed through her door, she was prepared (or as prepared as anyone can be) to experience a "radical respect for the humanity" of her assailant.[18] Likewise, as a lifelong disciple of Christ, Dallin Oaks was also prepared. Decades of service and charity conditioned him to interpret the crisis with the young assailant in ways that others might not have imagined. In both cases, years of selfless stretching and discipline prepared these remarkable people to recognize their divine interrelatedness when it counted most— when other people were threatening them with significant harm. If they hadn't already been outwardly oriented, they probably wouldn't have recognized the awakening when it was offered. Fortunately, both of them did, averting conflict, violence, and damage—a *shared* damage.

Developing an Affiliation Reflex

Because we can rarely predict exactly when or how a conflict or threat will emerge, we have to simply train ourselves to respond reflexively. In modern combat training, soldiers are conditioned to fire their guns instinctively by pulling the trigger thousands of times in fast and intensive drills. Likewise, we can develop an "affiliation reflex," where we learn to instinctively react as the prophet Jacob suggested—to think of our brethren, even our enemies, "like unto ourselves."[19] And as is the case in learning to fire a gun, we learn to employ weapons of love through repetition, repetition, and more repetition—training our emotional reflexes

---

18 O'Gorman, *The Universe Bends Towards Justice*, 243–244.
19 See Jacob 2:17.

to jump automatically to our interconnectedness. One way we might do this is to exercise our emotional muscles by deliberately remembering the divine connections and spiritual parentage we share with those we find most difficult to love—the violent killer who so mercilessly hurts young and innocent people, the coworker whose motives and ambitions we suspect, the politician with whom we fiercely disagree, the family member who said or did such damaging things.

As with any skill, some people have a natural talent for recognizing and reestablishing divine associations. All of us probably know someone who seems to effortlessly connect with other people. But the rest of us have to practice. And, as with any skill I've tried to develop, when I try to stretch my emotional muscles, I find that some attempts seem effortless while others are hard work. Sometimes I can bridge the emotional distance and feel the connection. Sometimes I can't. But I keep trying to bend my heart in the right direction, to practice an inclination to connect, to discover a sincere regard for the shared safety and fate of the people around me—especially those I find hardest to love.

With God's help we can do it. But we have to exert the effort. And while we should never neglect practicing love for those "enemies" who may be distant from us, it is in the laboratory of our most intimate relations where we have the opportunity to most fully practice and condition these reflexes. Clearly perceiving and genuinely expressing our divine affiliations can be challenging, even in situations where it seems as if it should be easy, such as our families. As I try to remember and reinforce these deep connections with my wife and children, not all of my efforts are successful. At the right moment, with the right look, word, or touch, I feel the connection strengthening, but I cannot conjure these moments as easily or as predictably as I would prefer, because I am constantly fighting my own insecurities and selfish tendencies. If I relate to my wife or son or daughter with any degree of self-interest (out of a desire to be "right" or in any way protect my own comfort or pride), no matter how I try to package or convey my actions, they will play false—because they are. And even when my motives are essentially pure, my love doesn't always hit its mark, and a divine connection isn't strengthened as much as I might wish.

I once attended a conference in Baltimore near the Inner Harbor. It was my first experience in that city, and I loved it. My hotel was quaint, with an antique elevator and an architecturally unique room.

In the evenings as I walked the harbor, visited art museums, and ate delicious meals, I kept thinking how much my wife would have enjoyed the hotel, the docks, the art, the food—and how much I would have enjoyed sharing those moments with her. On my last evening we had a long conversation on the phone. As I lay on my hotel bed listening to her voice, I remembered similar conversations with her when we were engaged. I was living in Minnesota at the time, and Dawn was in Utah. We spent hours suspended on an aural tether strung between the two states. Now we were doing it again, and I relaxed into the pillows as I listened to her recount her day. Before we hung up, we each said, "I love you," as we always do. Then I drifted off to sleep.

The next morning we spoke again, and Dawn told me how touched she had been by my expression of love the night before. "Why?" I asked.

"I don't know," she replied. "There was just something in your voice. It was so sincere and heartfelt. I was moved."

I hadn't *tried* to be sincere or heartfelt. But I had *felt* a deep connection to her as we spoke, and somehow, serendipitously, unconsciously, I had bridged the distance and communicated that divine association through my voice. Since then, I have tried to recapture the magic of that moment. Every day I tell Dawn how much I love her. And she knows that I do. But I have never managed to fully re-create the effect. Perhaps I have tried too hard. Such moments can't be forced. Angie O'Gorman couldn't have forced her divine connection. Neither could Dallin Oaks. Or my mother. Such moments just come—if we prepare ourselves.

Dawn and I have had other subsequent experiences—a look, a touch, a smile, an act of service—that have reinforced our divine connection, and all of them have been similarly unexpected and delightful. So I keep working on my love and connections, imagining them, practicing them, expressing them, because I want to be ready when the gifts of such moments arrive. And not just with my wife, with whom I am rarely in conflict. I want to be ready when it really counts, facing some unpredictable threat or danger or anger, whether it comes from an intruder in the night or while I am standing in a checkout lane at the supermarket. However it happens, I want the love and connections I have practiced to trigger an "affiliation reflex." I want to be open to gifts of humanity and connection and then act out of concern for my "enemies," whoever they may be, so all of us can emerge from that confrontation safe and secure in some divinely appointed future.

Chapter 7
PLANNING TO BE SURPRISED

A SPECTER OF VIOLENCE ONCE haunted the Southern states. Periodic lynching—of mostly young black men—reinforced a strict segregation system. The pattern was predictable. Each time one or more African-Americans tried to assert their equality or cross racial lines, an explosive act of violence—a hanging in the town square, perhaps—would remind the black community that such encroachments were unacceptable. Many white Southerners abhorred the system, but the violence intimidated them as well. So they kept silent, yielding to the extreme behavior of a few people and quietly allowing the system to perpetuate itself.

In the late 1950s and early 60s, the pattern was interrupted. African-Americans began to employ weapons of love to break the destructive cycle of intimidation, to disarm their adversaries, and to achieve the basic equality to which they were entitled. One of the most effective leaders in this effort was a young minister named James Lawson, who moved to Nashville in 1959 with the intention of challenging and over-throwing the city's system of segregation. Lawson was a deeply commit-ted Christian, and he believed assertive love could break the system. But he was no starry-eyed idealist trusting in some nebulous mystical force to accomplish this goal. He had a plan. In contrast to many people who haphazardly try to employ love to overcome hate, Lawson recognized the importance of "training and strategizing and planning and recruit-ing and doing the kinds of things you do to have a movement." But "That can't happen spontaneously," he later noted. "It has to be done systematically."[20] Which is exactly what he did.

---

20 James Lawson, in *A Force More Powerful*, directed by Steve York (York Zimmerman, 2000), DVD.

He began by holding workshops in the basement of a local church. At first only a handful of students from the local black colleges attended. But as the audacity of their plans and the power of Lawson's ideas began to leak out, the workshops began to attract more and more people. Their goal was to desegregate Nashville, but they needed an appropriate place to start—something that would attract allies from the larger black community. They decided to focus on lunch counters in department stores where blacks were allowed to shop but not eat—a grating symbol of their second-class status. "That was the first step," Lawson noted, "to research and examine and focus on an issue—choose a target."[21]

Next he prepared his troops for battle. "You cannot go on a demonstration with twenty-five people doing whatever they want to do. They have to have a common discipline."[22] The strategy was to sit at the lunch counters, politely ask for service, and refuse to leave when they were denied. Such a breach of social norms was sure to antagonize some people, who might lash out at them. Lawson wanted them to be prepared, so he staged little "sociodramas" to help them anticipate what would happen. One of his pupils, John Lewis, described how the training worked:

> Several of us would sit in a row of folding chairs, acting out a sit-in, while the others played waitresses or angry bystanders, calling us niggers, cursing in our faces, pushing and shoving us to the floor. Always James Lawson would be there, hovering over the action, pushing, prodding, teaching, cajoling. It was not enough, he would say, simply to endure a beating. It was not enough to resist the urge to strike back at an assailant. "That urge can't *be* there," he would tell us. "You have to do more than just not hit back. You have to have no *desire* to hit back. You have to *love* that person who's hitting you. You're *going* to love him."[23]

Throughout the training, Lewis remembered that Lawson stressed that assertive love was "not simply a technique or a tactic or a strategy or a tool to be pulled out when needed"—it was a way of life. "It is not something you turn on and off like a faucet. This sense of love, this sense of peace, the capacity for compassion, is something you carry inside yourself every waking minute of the day."[24]

---

21 Ibid.
22 Ibid.
23 John Lewis, *Walking with the Wind: A Memoir of the Movement* (New York: Simon and Schuster, 1998), 93, emphasis in the original.
24 Ibid., 86.

We talked a lot about the idea of "redemptive suffering" . . . It affects not only ourselves, but it touches and changes those around us as well. It opens us and those around us to a force beyond ourselves, a force that is right and moral, the force of righteous truth that is the basis of all human conscience. Suffering puts us and those around us in touch with our consciences. It opens and touches our hearts. . . .

We are talking about love here. Not romantic love. Not the love of one individual for another. Not loving something that is lovely to you. This is a broader, deeper, more all-encompassing love. It is a love that accepts and embraces the hateful and the hurtful. It is a love that recognizes the spark of the divine in each of us, even in those who would raise their hand against us, those we might call our enemy.[25]

Lawson was steeling them for battle, teaching them to restrain their natural impulses to give in or strike back, and suggesting ways they might establish a connection with their adversaries. Through these scenarios Lawson created an army of forcefully loving soldiers. "We were warriors," one participant later observed, describing Lawson's rigorous workshops as "a nonviolent academy, equivalent to West Point."[26] And when the day came to implement their plans, the operation had become as complex, disciplined, and tightly organized as any military campaign:

The students doing the actual sitting-in would have an entire logistical system behind them. There would be drivers to take participants from campuses to the First Baptist Church, which would be the staging area and control center. There would be people at the church keeping track of who was where and what was happening downtown, and there would be monitors and runners in the downtown streets, relaying information back to the church and instructions to the protesters in the stores. And there would be people assigned to deal with the press.[27]

On the first day of the sit-ins, groups of young people went to several prominent stores, sat at the counters, and were denied service, as expected. When the students remained at the counters, they caught the

25 Ibid., 85–86.

26 Bernard Lafayette, in *A Force More Powerful*, DVD, directed by Steve York (York Zimmerman, 2000).

27 Peter Ackerman and Jack DuVall, *A Force More Powerful: A Century of Nonviolent Conflict* (New York: St. Martin's Press, 2000), 317.

business owners completely off guard. They weren't acting as the owners expected. They weren't being rude, but neither were they giving in to the abusive segregation system. So the owners closed the counters and turned off the lights, but the students remained in their seats reading and studying until evening when the main parts of the department stores closed.

No violence occurred that day, nor on the second or third day of sit-ins, although white protesters and taunting thugs steadily increased in number and intensity. But as the fourth day approached, the sit-in leaders learned that the police planned to pull out of the downtown area and let the thugs have their way. As the students sat down at the lunch counters, they were assaulted—pulled from their stools, kicked and beaten, doused with mustard or ketchup—but not a single student fought back. James Lawson had trained his soldiers well.

The police finally returned and began arresting the students instead of their assailants. With silent dignity, the students allowed themselves to be arrested and escorted into police wagons. Then, to everyone's surprise, another rank of students quietly took their place at the lunch counters. The officers didn't know what to do. These polite, well-dressed young people were not afraid of jail. They could not be intimidated nor goaded into fighting. Those who went to jail gently but firmly refused to pay bail or fines, even reduced ones, forcing the city to either incarcerate them— to great national embarrassment, as the facts started to get out—or let them go. Mayor Ben West chose the latter.

Some of the city's ardent segregationists stepped up their tactics. They forced the expulsion of James Lawson (considered to be a meddling "outsider") from the Vanderbilt School of Divinity, where he had been studying. But as white intimidation increased, so did black solidarity. Bolstered by the examples of these young loving warriors, the entire black community began a boycott of downtown stores. Many whites also stayed away. "It was a ghost town down there," one student remembered.[28] Consequently, many store owners wanted to change the policies but didn't want to be the first to introduce such radical changes to a social system that had been in force for generations.

As the impasse dragged on for several weeks, some segregationists resorted to extreme measures. Early one morning they bombed the home of a prominent black lawyer who had defended the students. No one was seriously hurt, but the violence created an unexpected opportunity

---

28 Ibid., 324.

for the students. They quickly organized a march for later that day. It was a silent march through the heart of the black community (where the march swelled to 4,000 participants) to the steps of city hall. Mayor Ben West came out to meet them, and the confrontation did not begin well:

> C. T. Vivian, a fiery black minister who had participated in the workshops and sit-ins, excoriated the mayor for not speaking out against the violence and said that his police force had not upheld the law. West was offended, got into a heated argument with Vivian, and told the protesters about all the good things he had done for black people. At that point, Diane Nash [one of the student leaders] spoke up. Rather than attack West, she appealed to his sense of fairness . . . asking the mayor if he felt "that it's wrong to discriminate against a person solely on the basis of his race or color." West tried "to answer it frankly and honestly," he said later. "I could not agree that it was morally right for someone to sell them merchandise and refuse them service." Then she asked if he thought the lunch counters should be desegregated. First he hemmed and hawed, but Nash was not going to let him off the hook, and she asked again: "Then, Mayor, do you recommend that the lunch counters be desegregated?" West, finally, said "Yes." The crowd erupted in applause, and West and the protestors hugged each other.[29]

With the mayor's blessing, department store owners began to secretly tell the students that they wanted to desegregate their lunch counters. James Lawson remembered the students' response: "We suggested to [the store owners]—which was a great relief to them—that there would be no announcement that the demonstrations had ended. There would be no announcements that black people were being served. No announcements. No press. No police."[30] Quietly, yet systematically, the lunch counters were desegregated, and the entire community (white and black) began to heal. The students sought neither recognition for themselves nor humiliation for their opponents. They started the campaign with assertive love, and they ended it the same way—open to the humanity of their former enemies, many of whom were now their friends. The rest of the city (theatres, restaurants, and other public facilities) desegregated within a few years.

29 Ibid., 326–327.
30 Lawson, in *A Force More Powerful*, DVD, directed by Steve York (York Zimmerman, 2000).

Systematic Strategizing

The pivotal moment came when Diane Nash reawakened and established a divine connection with Mayor West. Being respectful and open to the gift of *his* humanity, her questions—gentle but firm and probing—invited him to consider the gift of *her* humanity, and the humanity of the people she represented. The moment surprised both Nash and West. Neither expected it to happen the way it did—on the steps of city hall with a crowd watching and cameras rolling. But, as James Lawson pointed out, such moments don't just "happen spontaneously." While they cannot be forced, they can and must be *encouraged*. Creating a "context of conversion," an environment in which such moments have a better chance of occurring, takes "training and strategizing and planning." As Lawson said, "It has to be done systematically."

The same is true for our more intimate conflicts. While sudden violence (such as a mugging or an explosive customer) may require a spontaneous response of assertive love, such reflexes can only be built through previous and consistent practice with the principles of forgiveness, charity, and divine connectedness. Over weeks, months, years, even decades, we must consistently train ourselves, as did the students in Lawson's workshops, to be open to the gift of other people's humanity, to respond to anger and aggression with assertive love. As Charles Penrose wrote:

> School thy feelings, O my brother;
> Train thy warm, impulsive soul.
> Do not its emotions smother,
> But let wisdom's voice control.
> School thy feelings; there is power
> In the cool, collected mind.
> Passion shatters reason's tower,
> Makes the clearest vision blind. . . .
> Noblest minds have finest feelings;
> Quiv'ring strings a breath can move;
> And the gospel's sweet revealings
> Tune them with the key of love.[31]

Through conscientious practice and effort, we "tune" our "finest feelings" to the "key of love." And as our hearts and heads become more

---

31 Charles W. Penrose, "School Thy Feelings," *Hymns* (Salt Lake City: The Church of Jesus Christ of Latter-day Saints, 1985), no. 336.

finely tuned, we become more and more apt to reflexively respond to sudden and unexpected anger and aggression with forceful kindness.

Some forms of violence and aggression are not sudden and unexpected. They are chronic and perpetual. Racial segregation in the South was a chronic system of violence. So are many of our more intimate relationships—a hostile work environment, a family plagued by abuse, or any strained friendship. In such chronic systems, the *general* anger or aggression is not surprising—in fact, those who regularly experience such relationships usually walk on eggshells, constantly anticipating the next outburst—although *specific* violent incidents still usually catch people off guard. Employing assertive love in such chronic situations requires more than simply training our reflexes. It can require a formal assault on the fundamental dynamic of the relationship. Such assaults, as the one on Nashville's racial segregation, take time, rigorous preparation, systematic planning, careful implementation, and sometimes even allies.

My wife belongs to a circle of friends who became concerned with one of their members. Tracy was a warm, energetic, and sparkling woman who had a way of lifting everyone around her. Her husband, Tyler, was generous, scrupulous, and loyal, a man everyone respected and enjoyed for his quick wit. But soon after their marriage, Tyler began to criticize Tracy—her attitude, her appearance, her personality—and over the years his private comments grew increasingly acerbic and his language more coarse and relentless.

As the years passed, the abuse took its toll—psychologically, emotionally, and physically. Behind Tracy's brave smiles, she clearly carried the pain of her burden. She grew increasingly and uncharacteristically reclusive, reluctant to meet friends and acquaintances, who always seemed shocked by her transformation. On several occasions, the marriage almost collapsed. But despite her deep wounds, Tracy continued to exhibit remarkable strength, retained an exceptional ability to love and forgive, and remained committed to their marriage, come what may. Professional counseling gave her tools to diffuse combustible situations, but the daily struggles often seemed greater than she could bear.

Having watched from the sidelines with occasional but only sporadically successful interventions, her friends decided their irregular efforts were not enough. They needed to engage in a more systematic and coordinated effort to help their besieged friend—and to help Tyler. For although they had often been frustrated by the situation, all of them still loved Tyler and wanted to act in a way that would help create a context for conversion and mutual healing. After getting wind of a particularly nasty blow-up, one of the friends, Joanne, sent an e-mail to the others calling for collective action (which I quote with her permission):

> Tracy is one of my heroes. She is amazing and resilient and one of the most genuinely loving people that I know. In the last two days she came by and stopped and talked for a little bit, and she's been remarkably open about how hard her situation is, how tired she is of the struggle, etc. I worry for her, my heart breaks at hearing specific struggles, and I long for her to know the safety of a healthy, good marriage. But I feel hope that the true Tracy is up to the challenge. How can we help her be her best, strongest, wisest, most spiritually-in-tune self?
>
> Tracy deserves an organized effort to help her. I have no idea what lies within our sphere of influence, but I want to try to figure it out. I think the true Tracy would always have made any sacrifice to help save a soul, and it looks like that's what she doing now with Tyler. But there must be some way in which we can give coordinated support to her struggle and to help her in more deliberate ways. There are souls at stake here. Tracy. Tyler. The children. They all need our best effort.

For several weeks (and with Tracy's blessing, though not her participation) my wife's circle of friends discussed various strategies they might implement. They fasted. They prayed. They candidly expressed and assessed patterns and possibilities. Whatever strategy they implemented, they knew it had to be sustainable for months, years, perhaps even indefinitely. In the end they settled on a two-pronged approach. First, they knew they needed to call upon the powers of heaven, so they decided that in each of their daily prayers and their monthly fasts they would pray for Tracy and Tyler in very specific ways—that they would be able to overcome the anger and abuse and build bonds of love and trust. These prayers and fasts served two purposes. They helped marshal spiritual power on behalf of the couple, but perhaps even better, they also helped these friends develop greater love and forgiveness as they earnestly prayed for *both* people.

This first prong was crucial for the other part of their strategy—to regularly and consistently demonstrate and express love for both Tracy and Tyler. This was the tangible aspect of their strategy. They knew that prayer was efficacious but not enough. They needed to implement practical behaviors that would build their friend and her husband and strengthen their marriage. The friends had noticed that when Tracy's relationship with Tyler became particularly stressful, she would withdraw from both her friends and her therapist, leaving her more isolated and vulnerable. Conversely, the times when she was best able to lovingly resist anger and aggression was when she was surrounded and supported by a strong social and professional network. So they resolved to each maintain consistent contact—weekly, at least—to find ways to openly express their faith in and love for her, to help her keep her professional appointments, and to consistently remind her of the army of loving soldiers at her back. Because some members of the group lived in other states, they decided to use e-mails, phone calls, and social networking tools to share uplifting thoughts and expressions of support. In addition, although they did not interact with him as regularly, each friend committed to seize every opportunity to demonstrate love and kindness to Tyler. Finally, because any army—even a loving one—requires coordination and accountability, the group decided that once a month they would report on their activities, share their observations, and discuss their progress or changes of strategy.

With these plans in hand and on a day when everyone was in town, Dawn's circle of friends took Tracy to lunch and presented their ideas to her. She wept at their expression of love. They wept as well, sharing their love, faith, and commitment to help. Then, with everyone on board and with their marching orders, this loving army left the restaurant and put their carefully constructed battle plan into motion.

And things got better. A few weeks after the lunch, Tracy's marriage hit a new crisis, but with the strength of a loving army at her back, she didn't retreat. She stood firm—gently but forcefully resisting Tyler's anger and aggression. And he responded. Not immediately, but over the ensuing months, the anger and aggression slowly subsided in intensity. And in its wake, tender shoots of love and trust began to emerge. Rather than dreading Tyler's return from work each night, Tracy began to look forward to his companionship. Not everything was perfect. Nor did it always improve at a steady rate. But their love was stronger. Their trust was deeper. Their marriage was better and headed in the right direction. Her friends continued to implement their strategy and kept it going over months, even years. Certain elements still remain in force and will for perhaps the rest of their lives.

Such methodical and systematic plans, as exhibited by my wife's circle of friends and James Lawson's workshops, do not preclude sincerity. In fact, such planning and implementation makes sincere love all the more important. Assaulting and overcoming any destructive dynamic requires sincere love and forgiveness. Without sincerity, any effort we make will be hollow and hypocritical. James Lawson's students found love and strength in the Bible. My wife's friends cultivated it through fasting and prayer. Seeking this gift is essential. When we take on chronic anger and aggression, we desperately need the gift of God's love and forgiveness, the capacity to be open to the humanity of people with whom we have been in perpetual conflict, because often the chronic nature of the conflict has worn us down and we have become suspicious in ways that make loving and being truly open to these people very difficult. In our systematic strategizing, we need God's love. And if we ask, He will provide.

We don't necessarily need an army to plan and implement successful loving resistance. All we need is courage, conviction, and creativity. We can be an army of one. And as an army of one, we can establish effective battle plans—carefully crafting strategies of loving resistance, practicing methods for gently standing firm against anger, implementing tactics for sincerely reaching out to our "enemies." But of course, we are never really alone. God will always be our general, if we let Him.

Letting the Spirit Take Control

Even after all of the training and strategizing and planning, even after carefully and systematically implementing meticulously crafted battle plans, there comes a time in every conflict when we must let go and trust the dynamics of love—the reliable, tangible, forceful dynamics of love—to work their art. We cannot plan for every contingency or anticipate every response. Similar to a soldier in a traditional war, we must walk into battle as prepared as we can be but not knowing exactly what will happen. This isn't to suggest we can't or shouldn't plan. We should. But in the end, we must trust our training, our companions (both divine and mortal), our strategies, and our weaponry—love. John Lewis, who built on his experience as a student in Nashville to lead other forcefully loving campaigns against segregation, described the paradoxical feelings of power and uncertainty that prefaced every conflict in which he engaged, even after years of experience:

You feel a mixture of fear and excitement. There's a stirring inside as well, the sense of a power beyond you, of a calling, a mission. That's a strong feeling, and it does help calm the soul.

But doubts linger, the feeling of not knowing what to expect. . . . It's different every time. It's dangerous every time. It's more real and more vividly gripping than any experience I can imagine. And it's totally unpredictable. You can prepare and make plans, but in the end you have to hand it over to the spirit, just let the spirit take control.[32]

As we plan and employ our forcefully loving strategies, we must ultimately be open to serendipity. Because such strategies necessarily involve moral agency on the part of the other party, no one can predict or coerce a particular outcome. We help create a context for conversion then stand back, wait, and watch. And as does an army in a traditional battle, we must usually adapt our strategies to changing circumstances. As a great general once noted: "No plan of operations extends with certainty beyond the first encounter with the enemy's main strength."[33] But in contrast to a traditional army, which adjusts by constantly probing to find and exploit the enemy's weakest points, an army of love adjusts by seeking and seizing serendipitous opportunities to establish divine connections or by exploiting unexpected moments in which gifts of humanity might be exchanged.

The Book of Mormon describes several carefully crafted and executed plans of loving resistance in which the participants flexibly adapted to the changing circumstances, taking advantage of unexpected opportunities for divine connections. The sons of Mosiah, for example, carefully "selected" other loving warriors and organized themselves before they journeyed into the territory of their traditional enemies, the Lamanites.

There comes a time in every conflict when we must let go and trust the dynamics of love . . . to work their art.

But these missionaries did not think of the Lamanites as their enemies. The sons of Mosiah were open to the gift of their brethren's humanity, and before teaching, these young men prepared themselves to love—"they

---

32 Lewis, *Walking with the Wind*, 101.
33 Helmuth Karl Bernhard Graf von Moltke, in *Moltke on the Art of War: Selected Writings*, ed. Daniel J. Hughes (New York: Presidio Press, 1993), 45.

fasted much and prayed much that the Lord would grant unto them a portion of his Spirit to go with them, and abide with them, that they might be an instrument in the hands of God to bring, if it were possible, their brethren, the Lamanites, to the knowledge of the truth."[34]

The Lord, in turn, taught the sons of Mosiah key principles regarding weapons of love, telling them to "be patient in long-suffering and afflictions, that ye may show forth good examples unto them in me, and I will make an instrument of thee in my hands unto the salvation of many souls."[35] Having accepted this direction, Ammon "did administer unto them" and "blessed them according to their several stations." Then the group separated themselves, "invading" their enemies' territory and confronting them with assertive love. They did not sit and wait. They acted.

But at this point, after all their carefully crafted plans and preparations, they became as John Lewis, and "just let the spirit take control." Ammon proved particularly adept at this, submitting himself to King Lamoni but watching for and seizing opportunities to connect with his former enemies—first at the waters of Sebus when he defended the king's flocks, then when he was summoned for an audience before Lamoni, and later with Lamoni's father when Ammon recognized the chance to demonstrate his love.[36]

About seventeen years later, Ammon joined Alma on another well-organized resistance effort, this time to the apostate Zoramites, who were beginning to break away from the Nephites and threatening to open correspondence with hostile Lamanites. In the face of this threat, Alma decided confrontational love was more powerful than violence (and he was no stranger to war): "And now, as the preaching of the word had a great tendency to lead the people to do that which was just—yea, it had had more powerful effect upon the minds of the people than the sword, or anything else, which had happened unto them—therefore Alma thought it was expedient that they should try the virtue of the word of God."[37]

As Ammon and his brethren had done with their mission to the Lamanites, Alma handpicked his loving warriors, trained them, blessed them, and then sent them on their way, each surrendering himself to the

---

34 Alma 17:9.
35 Alma 17:6–18.
36 See Alma 17–20.
37 Alma 31:5.

guidance of the Holy Ghost: "And . . . they did separate themselves one from another, taking no thought for themselves what they should eat, or what they should drink, or what they should put on. And the Lord provided for them that they should hunger not, neither should they thirst; yea, and he also gave them strength, that they should suffer no manner of afflictions, save it were swallowed up in the joy of Christ."[38] With firm but gentle truth, they confronted the subtle aggression of the Zoramites, and they watched carefully for opportunities to establish divine connections. Alma experienced an unexpected opening as he preached on the hill Onidah. As he spoke to one group, another group approached him with humble questions. Sensing a window had suddenly opened, he changed course, turning around and delivering one of the most eloquent and hopeful sermons in the Book of Mormon. Many were touched by his expression of love and were converted.[39]

Surprised by Deliverance

Although we hope—fervently hope—that we can establish a divine connection by meeting anger and aggression with assertive love (whether as individuals or as a group), the truly remarkable thing about wielding a weapon of love is that even if conversion does not happen, *we are still more free than before*. Let me repeat that, because it is crucial. Even if our so-called enemies are not touched or converted in any way by our love, *we are still more free than before*—free from anger, free from fear, free from their unrighteous influence in our lives—and the power of their anger and aggression are substantially diminished, if not completely neutralized.

This principle is perhaps best illustrated by an extreme example. No system could seem more immune to the effects of assertive love than Adolf Hitler's Third Reich in the 1930s and 40s, and yet the history of German occupation in Europe is rife with examples of how Nazi brutality was countered, even rendered impotent, by gentle but firm resistance. In Norway, for example, the fascist government tried to set up a tightly controlled curriculum of propaganda in the national school system, but the teachers refused to cooperate. When the government announced a new compulsory teacher's organization and fascist youth movement, the underground resistance movement called on teachers to resist, providing form letters protesting the new organization and

38 Alma 31:37–38.
39 See Alma 32.

refusing membership. Between 8,000 to 10,000 teachers (out of 12,000) signed their names to the letters and sent them to the government.

Each teacher said he (or she) could neither assist in promoting fascist education of the children nor accept membership in the new teachers' organization.

The government threatened them with dismissal and then closed all schools for a month. Teachers held classes in private homes. Despite censorship, news of the resistance spread. Tens of thousands of letters of protest from parents poured into the government office.

After the teachers defied the threats, about one thousand male teachers were arrested and sent to concentration camps. Children gathered and sang at the railroad stations as teachers were shipped in cattle cars. In the camps, the Gestapo imposed an atmosphere of terror to induce capitulation. On starvation rations, the teachers were put through "torture gymnastics" in deep snow. When only a few gave in, "treatment" continued.

The schools reopened, but the teachers still at liberty told their pupils they repudiated membership in the new organization and spoke of a duty of conscience. Rumors were spread that if these teachers did not give in, some or all of those arrested would be killed. After difficult inner wrestling, the teachers who had not been arrested almost without exception stood firm.[40]

The fascist government had tried to intimidate the teachers into compliance, but they refused to be intimidated. And by refusing to be intimidated, they rendered the government helpless. In fact, at one point, the Minister-President yelled at the teachers in a school near the capital: "You teachers have destroyed everything for me!"[41] Afraid of losing even more popular support, he released the male teachers, and Hitler advised him to drop the program altogether. Consequently, although the fascist regime had not been converted and repented of its oppressive tactics, its power had been diminished—and by nothing more than weapons of love, consisting of courage, resolve, and a quiet but firm resistance to violence and aggression.

When weapons of love are grounded in sincerity and truth and when they are carefully and systematically employed, they achieve one

---

40 Gene Sharp, *The Politics of Nonviolent Action, Part One: Power and Struggle* (Boston: Extending Horizon Books, 1973), 88.
41 Ibid., 89.

of two liberating outcomes—either they convert a so-called enemy into a friend, or else they diminish or neutralize the raw power of anger and aggression, frustrating those who would use such tactics to influence other people. Thus one of the most surprising aspects of assertive love is that when we effectively wield it, *we can't really lose.* It's a double-lucky coin toss. Heads? We win. Tails? We win.

This principle of deliverance—regardless of the outcome, regardless of the choices our "enemies" make—is beautifully illustrated by three courageous Hebrew youth—Shadrach, Meshach, and Abed-nego. Confronted with a brutal edict to bow down before Nebuchadnezzar's golden idol or be thrown into a fiery furnace, they chose loving resistance and refused to bow. When Nebuchadnezzar heard of their resistance, he demanded in "rage and fury" that they obey the edict or be consumed by the flames.

Even if our so-called enemies are not touched or converted in any way by our love, we are still more free than before—free from anger, free from fear, free from their unrighteous influence in our lives.

With gentle courage, Shadrach, Meshach, and Abed-nego stood up to the king and said, "If it be so, our God whom we serve is able to deliver us from the burning fiery furnace, and he will deliver us out of thine hand, O king. But if not, be it known unto thee, O king, that we will not serve thy gods, nor worship the golden image which thou hast set up."[42]

As we know, God did rescue them from the flames. However, the key to their resistance was a small phrase—"But if not." So much power, so much liberty, in just a few words. Perhaps God would miraculously save them. Perhaps not. It didn't really matter. Even if they died, they were delivered. Either way, they would not submit to Nebuchadnezzar's threats and violence. Either way, they were free of his unrighteous influence. Either way, the power of his anger and aggression was diminished. They knew it. He knew it. Which is why he railed with such "rage and fury." But to no avail. The young Hebrews were free.

So it was with African-Americans. The moment they delivered themselves from racial segregation was not when whites acknowledged their rights but when they refused to be intimidated by the system. Fortunately, their white brethren and sisters recognized and corrected

---

42 Daniel 3:16–18.

their mistakes. Fortunately, a conversion occurred. But even if it hadn't, as long as African-Americans gently refused to be intimidated by threats or brutality, the system could not work. The power of anger and aggression was diminished. Both sides knew it. Which is why a few Southerners responded with dogs and cattle prods and fire hoses. But again, to no avail. African-Americans were free.

So it is with us. When we sincerely wield weapons of love against chronic anger and aggression—no matter what happens, no matter what our enemies choose—the dynamic changes in our favor. We will earnestly hope and work for conversion. We will extend every opportunity for healing and keep our hearts open to the gifts of their humanity, if they choose to accept our offer.

But if not, we are still free.

Epilogue
THE GREATEST FORCE

OVERLOOKING THE ICE-SKATING RINK AT Rockefeller Plaza in New York City is a large plaque inscribed with the credo of John D. Rockefeller Jr., a prominent philanthropist and the son of the famous industrialist. His credo consists of ten statements, each beginning with the words "I believe . . ." The very last statement reads: "I believe that love is the greatest thing in the world; that it alone can overcome hate; that right can and will triumph over might." I completely concur with this evaluation, except I would change two words. If I were to adopt such a credo, it would begin: "I believe love is the greatest *force* in the *universe*."

Love is powerful, but the principles upon which it operates are deceptively simple: Free-will beings like us are necessarily influenced by others. We cannot help it. Such connections are part of our eternal nature. Temporary influence can be achieved by intimidation or enticement, but abiding power can only be accomplished through mutual love and reciprocal trust cultivated by compassion and restraint. When we refuse to give in or retaliate against anger and aggression, we break destructive cycles of conflict that lamentably influence our peace and happiness. Through planning and practice, we can confront violence— even chronic violence—with assertive love, seeking opportunities to connect and convert, opening ourselves to the gift of our opponent's humanity, and diminishing the influence of anger and aggression.

These principles of assertive love are so simple. So elegant. So true. Still, at times they can seem so *hard* because they run solidly against the grain of our "natural man" tendencies, which are reinforced by our worldly training. As I try to implement these principles and infuse them into my soul, I am often frustrated by how easily I slip back into selfishness, how quickly I can succumb to fear, yield to aggression, or return anger for anger, even if it's only in my heart. At times I feel similar to Nephi when he exclaimed, "O wretched man that I am! Yea, my heart sorroweth because of my flesh; my soul grieveth because of mine iniquities. I am encompassed about, because of the temptations and the sins which do so easily beset me. . . . Why am I angry because of mine enemy?"[43]

I suppose there is some comfort in knowing that someone as exemplary as Nephi struggled with these principles. But what brings me even greater comfort is his declaration of hope, with which my heart fully resonates with words that could be my own: "Nevertheless, I know in whom I have trusted." As did Nephi, when "my heart groaneth because of my sins," I remember the moments when God has "been my support" and "led me through mine afflictions." Most of all, I remember when He has "filled me with his love."[44] I hearken back to that first recognizable experience with God's raw, abundant, and vibrant love— when it flooded my soul and enwrapped me in its divine possibilities. I recall subsequent times when His light and love seemed to lift and subsume me. And I remember that He has promised to fill me again if I pray "with all the energy of heart."[45]

These memories, promises, and principles give me hope. They offer glimpses of sublime potential and remind me of what might yet be—within myself and between others. And not in some ethereal or transcendent afterlife but here and now, in the gritty and tangible struggles that constitute so much of our daily experience. *This* is where we develop such talents. *Here* is the laboratory of our love, the schoolhouse of our charity where we learn to hone and harness its energies—then unleash them upon the world.

---

43 2 Nephi 4:17–27.
44 2 Nephi 4:19–21.
45 Moroni 7:48.

Bibliography

Ackerman, Peter, and Jack DuVall. *A Force More Powerful: A Century of Nonviolent Conflict.* New York: St. Martin's Press, 2000.

Bednar, David A. "In the Strength of the Lord," Devotional address delivered at Brigham Young University–Idaho, 8 January 2002.

La Boétie, Étienne de. *The Politics of Obedience: The Discourse of Voluntary Servitude.* Translated by Harry Kurz. Montreal: Black Rose Books, 1997.

Ellis, Joseph J. *His Excellency: George Washington.* New York: Alfred A. Knopf, 2005.

Eyes on the Prize: America's Civil Rights Movement, 1954-1985. Directed by Judith Vecchione. PBS, 2010. DVD.

Eyring, Henry B. "The Family." *Ensign.* February 1998.

A Force More Powerful. Directed by Steve York. York Zimmerman, 2000. DVD.

Frankl, Victor. *Man's Search for Meaning.* New York: Washington Square Press, 1985.

Frost, Robert. "Mending Wall." In *The Poetry of Robert Frost: The Collected Poems, Complete and Unabridged*, edited by Edward Connery Lathem. New York: Henry Holt and Company, 1969.

Gandhi, Mohandas K. *Harijan.* 24 February 1946.

———. *Non-Violence in Peace and War.* Vol. I. Ahmedabad: Navajivan Publishing House, 1948.

———. *Young India.* 30 June 1920.

Hinckley, Gordon B. "Excerpts from Recent Addresses of President Gordon B. Hinckley." *Ensign.* August 1996.

———. "Charity Never Faileth." *Ensign.* November 1981.

———. "An Ensign to the World." *Ensign.* November 2003.

Hughes, Daniel J., ed. *Moltke on the Art of War: Selected Writings.* New York: Presidio Press, 1993.

Kimball, Spencer W. "The False Gods We Worship." *Ensign.* June 1976.

King, Martin Luther, Jr. *A Testament of Hope: The Essential Writings and Speeches of Martin Luther King, Jr.* Edited by James M. Washington. San Francisco: HarperCollins, 1986.

Lewis, C. S. *The Weight of Glory and Other Addresses.* San Francisco: HarperCollins, 2001.

Lewis, John. *Walking with the Wind: A Memoir of the Movement.* New York: Simon and Schuster, 1998.

Lewis, Thomas, Fari Amini, and Richard Lannon. *A General Theory of Love.* New York: Vintage Books, 2000.

Liberty: The American Revolution. Directed by Ellen Hovde and Muffie Meyer. PBS Paramount, 2004. DVD.

Maxwell, Neal A. *Meek and Lowly.* Salt Lake City: Deseret Book, 1987.

Mitchell, Stephen, trans. *Tao Te Ching: A New English Version.* New York: HarperCollins, 1988.

Oaks, Dallin H. "Bible Stories and Personal Protection." *Ensign.* November 1992.

O'Gorman, Angie. "Defense Through Disarmament: Nonviolence and Personal Assault." In *The Universe Bends Toward Justice.* Edited by Angie O'Gorman. Philadelphia: New Society Publishers, 1990.

Penrose, Charles W. "School Thy Feelings." *Hymns.* Salt Lake City: The Church of Jesus Christ of Latter-day Saints, 1985. No. 336.

Peterson, Stanley A. "Contention Is Not of Me." Devotional address delivered at Brigham Young University–Idaho, 14 October 2003.

Sharp, Gene. *The Politics of Nonviolent Action, Part One: Power and Struggle.* Boston: Extending Horizon Books, 1973.

Teilhard de Chardin, Pierre. *Les directions de l'avenir*. Paris: Éditions du Seuil, 1973.

Templeton, Sir John. *Agape Love: A Tradition Found in Eight World Religions*. Philadelphia: Templeton Foundation Press, 1999.

Ten Boom, Corrie. *Tramp for the Lord*. With Jamie Buckingham. New York: Jove Books, 1978.

Thomas, Becky. "Don't model your parenting after Laman and Lemuel." *Mormon Times*. 24 January 2010.

Warner, Terry. *Bonds That Make Us Free: Healing Our Relationships, Coming to Ourselves*. Salt Lake City: Shadow Mountain, 2001.

The West. Directed by Stephen Ives. PBS Paramount, 2004. DVD.

Weintraub, Stanley. *Silent Night: The Story of the World War I Christmas Truce*. New York: Free Press, 2001.

Wink, Walter. *Jesus and Nonviolence: A Third Way*. Minneapolis: Fortress Press, 2003.

About the Author

FOR OVER TWO DECADES, DAVID Pulsipher has studied the links between faith, community, conflict, compassionate resistance, and assertive love. From his home base in the Upper Snake River Valley, where he teaches history at BYU–Idaho, his research has taken him around the world—to battlefields in the American South, to coal mines in southern Wales, to teeming cities in northern India—exploring the lives and patterns of some of the world's greatest loving warriors.